W9-BXM-474

Shop Drawings of Shaker Furniture and Woodenware

Volume 2

Measured Drawings
by Ejner Handberg

BERKSHIRE HOUSE PUBLISHERS

Lee, Massachusetts

Photographs by Jane McWhorter

SHOP DRAWINGS OF SHAKER FURNITURE AND WOODENWARE, VOL. 2
Copyright ©1975, 1991 by Ejner P. Handberg

All rights reserved. No part of this book may be used
or reproduced in any manner whatsoever without
written permission of Berkshire House Publishers,
480 Pleasant St., Suite 5, Lee, Massachusetts 01238.

ISBN 0-936399-18-X; previously ISBN 0-912944-29-3
Library of Congress No. 73-83797
Printed in the United States of America

17th Printing

PREFACE

This is not an attempt to write a book about the Shakers and their furniture. There are already excellent books which serve that purpose. I refer especially to those by Dr. and Mrs. Edward Deming Andrews. Rather, this is a collection of measured drawings made to scale and with dimensions and details accurately copied from Shaker pieces which have been in my shop for restoration or reproduction. These drawings and patterns have been accumulated over a period of many years of interest in the woodwork of the New England and New York State Shakers.

E.H.

1975

FOREWORD

Ejner (pronounced Eye' ner) Handberg was born in
Viborg, Denmark, in 1902. When he was seventeen, he moved
to New York. For most of his life, Ejner was a builder
in Berkshire County, Massachusetts.

His interest in working with wood began in boyhood
on his way to school, when every day he passed a shop
where a man worked at a lathe in the window. One of his
first jobs as a young man was building lead-lined
shipping crates for a Danish firm in New York that made
blueprint paper. As a builder, he was perhaps best known
for his addition to the handsome old Congregational Church
in Stockbridge, and for the studio in the same town that
he built for Norman Rockwell in a carriage shed that had
been stripped down to the frame.

Building was a way to make a living, according to
his wife Elsie, but Ejner's real love was cabinetwork.
In 1960, the Handbergs built the Pinewood Shop on
Route 102 in Lee, not far from Stockbridge, with a large
workshop for Ejner and a gift shop, where Elsie, who was
skilled in sewing, offered things that they made.

Ejner's involvement with Shaker furniture began with
a chance meeting with Faith and Edward Deming Andrews,
noted authorities on the Shakers and residents of
nearby Pittsfield. In search of a good cabinetmaker to
repair Shaker pieces and a good seamstress for a sewing
project, Dr. and Mrs. Andrews had been told of a husband and wife in Lee with those talents. They showed up
at the Handberg shop, and in spite of the fact that it
was not the Handbergs for whom the Andrewses had been
looking, the two couples hit it off.

The visit was the beginning of a friendship as well
as a working relationship. The Andrewses often stopped
by on Saturdays for tea and something Faith had baked,
frequently bringing Shaker furniture items for repair.
In the course of his work, and to satisfy his own interest, Ejner began to make lifesize measured drawings of
the pieces he handled, scouting the local dump for large
refrigerator and stove cartons to get cardboard big enough
for his work. In time, a thick stack of drawings accumulated.

Dr. and Mrs. Andrews, who appreciated the kind of understanding that results from the careful examination necessary to produce accurate drawings, urged the Handbergs to publish Ejner's work. The first book, published in 1973, by Berkshire Traveller Press was a family effort. Ejner redrew the pieces to a smaller scale, Elsie did the writing, and their daughter Anne typed the manuscript. Ejner and Elsie collaborated on the four Shaker books that followed, and a last book on measured drawings of 18th-century American furniture in 1983. Ejner died two years later.

Ejner Handberg's books have sold more widely than perhaps any other books on the Shakers. A large part of their appeal is their practical nature and their utter lack of pretense -- both, characteristics of Shaker work as well. Did Ejner appreciate the visual kinship between Shaker furniture and contemporary Danish design? No, says Elsie Handberg, adding that her husband didn't even like Danish Modern. Did the Handbergs develop a friendship with the few Shakers who remained at Hancock, Massachusetts, or New Lebanon, New York, as the Andrewses had? No, they didn't; Shaker furniture appealed to them in a way that the Shakers' way of life did not.

Today, Ejner Handberg's straightforward look at Shaker work continues to draw admirers into the Shaker sphere. I am grateful to Elsie Handberg and Anne Handberg Oppermann for insights and reminiscences.

June Sprigg, Curator
Hancock Shaker Village
Pittsfield, Massachusetts
1991

ACKNOWLEDGMENTS

This second book of *Shop Drawings of Shaker Furniture and Woodenware* includes pieces which have been in my shop, as well as several other interesting pieces from collections mentioned below.

Special thanks are due to Mrs. Edward Deming Andrews for permission to make measured drawings of several more pieces from the Andrews collection and for the help and information given me.

I am also very grateful for cooperation and for similar help and permission at Hancock Shaker Village, Hancock, Massachusetts and the Shaker Museum, Old Chatham, New York.

Although the Shaker cabinetmakers were obliged to make their furniture and woodenware with utility in mind, their work is eagerly sought today by museums and private collectors for its simplicity and beauty. I wish to thank several of these collectors for allowing me to examine and make drawings of Shaker pieces in their possession.

E.H.
1975

CONTENTS

NOTES TO THE CRAFTSMAN OR COLLECTOR

White pine was the most common wood used for furniture like cupboards, chests of drawers, benches, woodboxes and many other items.

Bedposts, chairposts and all parts requiring strength were usually made of hard maple or yellow birch.

Maple, birch and cherry were used for legs on trestle tables, drop leaf tables and stands. The tops were often pine. Square legs are tapered on the inner surfaces only.

Sometimes candlestands, work stands and sewing stands were made entirely of cherry, maple or birch. The legs are dovetailed to the shaft and the grain should run as nearly parallel to the general direction of the leg as possible. A thin metal plate should be fastened to the underside of the shaft and extend about three quarters of an inch along the base of each leg with a screw or nail put in the leg to keep them from spreading.

Parts for chairs and stools were mostly hard maple with an occasional chair made of curly or bird's-eye maple. Birch, cherry and butternut were used less often.

Oval boxes and carriers were nearly always made of maple. The bottoms and covers were fitted with quarter-sawn, edge-grain pine which is less apt to cup or warp than flat-grained boards. First the "fingers" or "lappers" are cut on the maple bands, then they are steamed and wrapped around an oval form and the fingers fastened with small copper or iron rivets (tacks). After they are dry and sanded the pine disks are fitted into the bottom and cover and fastened with small square copper or iron brads.

In New York State and New England, the woods used for the many different small pieces of cabinet work and woodenware were white pine, maple, cherry, yellow birch, butternut and native walnut. They were often finished with a coat of thin paint, or stained and varnished, or sometimes left with a natural finish.

"BEAUTY RESTS ON UTILITY"

WALL CLOCK
BY I. N. YOUNGS
HANCOCK SHAKER VILLAGE, HANCOCK MASS.

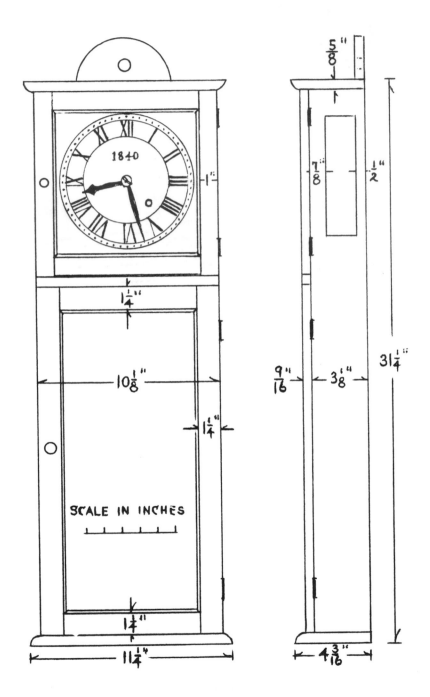

SCALE IN INCHES

WALL CLOCK
BY I. N. YOUNGS
HANCOCK SHAKER VILLAGE, HANCOCK MASS.

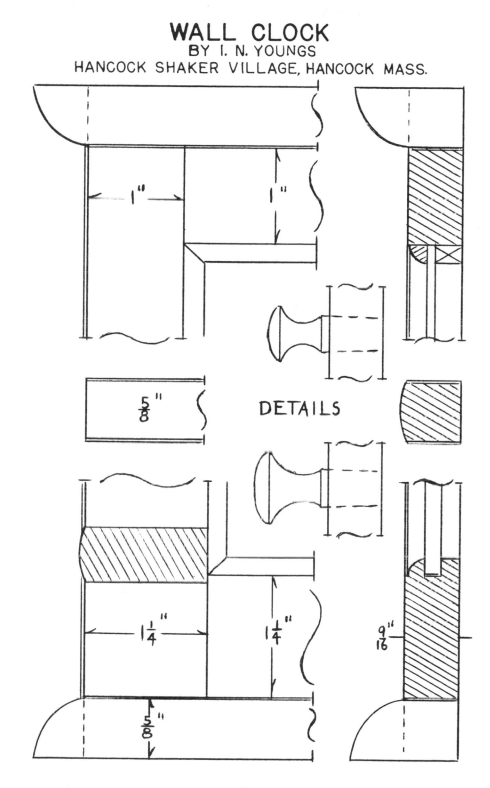

DETAILS

DESK
CHERRY

FROM ANDREWS
COLLECTION

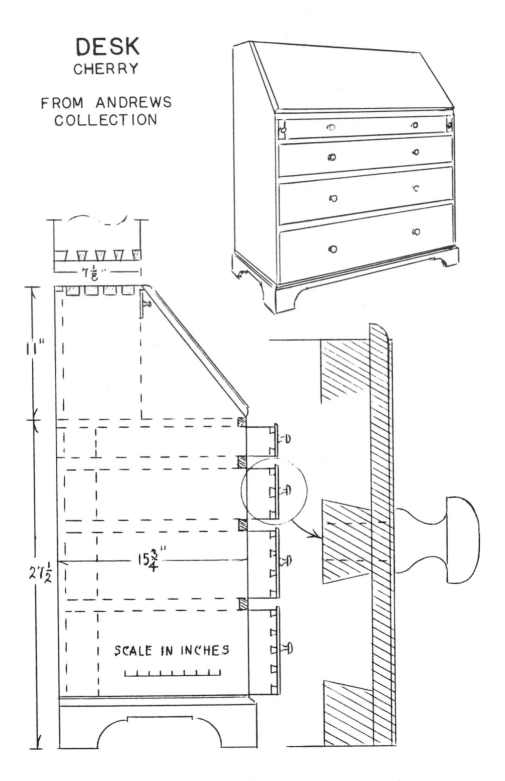

$7\frac{1}{8}$"

11"

$27\frac{1}{2}$"

$15\frac{3}{4}$"

SCALE IN INCHES

DESK
CHERRY

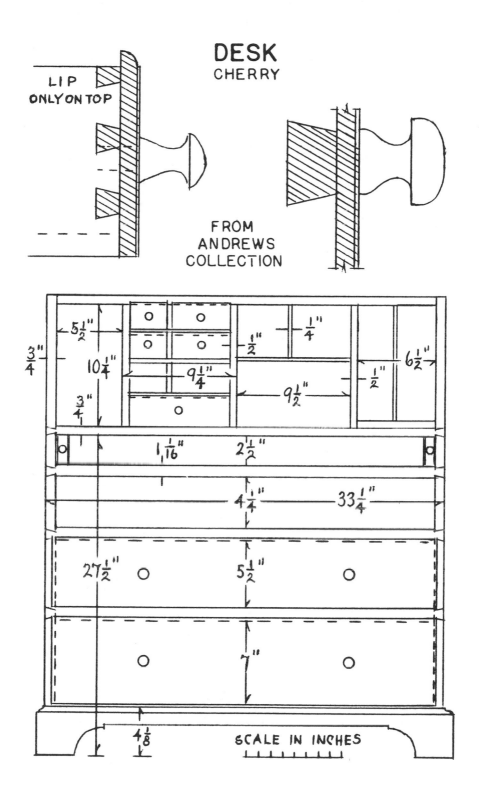

LIP
ONLY ON TOP

FROM
ANDREWS
COLLECTION

$5\frac{1}{2}$"

$\frac{3}{4}$"

$10\frac{1}{4}$"

$\frac{1}{2}$"

$\frac{1}{4}$"

$9\frac{1}{4}$"

$\frac{1}{2}$"

$9\frac{1}{2}$"

$6\frac{1}{2}$"

$\frac{1}{2}$"

$\frac{3}{4}$"

$1\frac{1}{16}$"

$2\frac{1}{2}$"

$4\frac{1}{4}$"

$33\frac{1}{4}$"

$27\frac{1}{2}$"

$5\frac{1}{2}$"

7"

$4\frac{1}{8}$"

SCALE IN INCHES

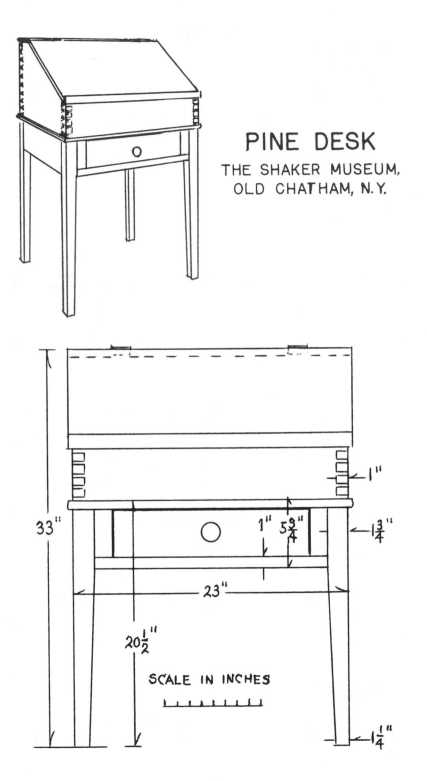

PINE DESK
THE SHAKER MUSEUM,
OLD CHATHAM, N.Y.

1"

1" 5$\frac{3}{4}$"

1$\frac{3}{4}$"

33"

23"

20$\frac{1}{2}$"

1$\frac{1}{4}$"

SCALE IN INCHES

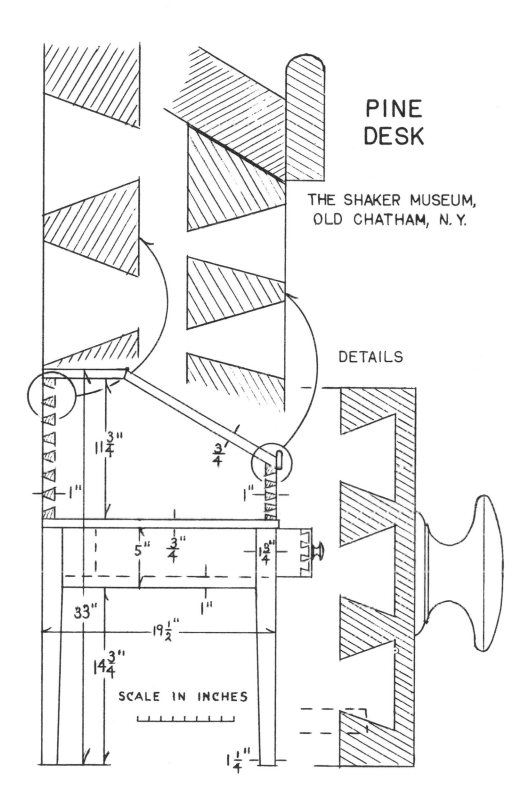

PINE
DESK

THE SHAKER MUSEUM,
OLD CHATHAM, N.Y.

DETAILS

SCALE IN INCHES

7

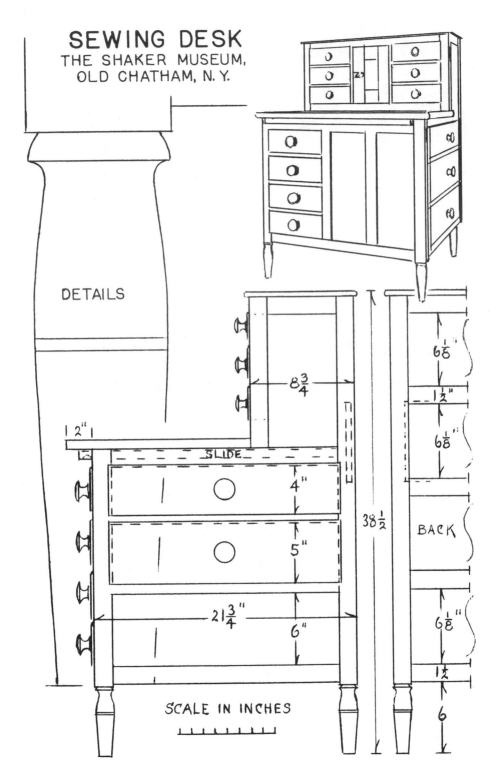

SEWING DESK
THE SHAKER MUSEUM,
OLD CHATHAM, N.Y.

DETAILS

SLIDE

$8\frac{3}{4}$

$1\,2''$

$4''$

$5''$

$21\frac{3}{4}''$

$6''$

$38\frac{1}{2}$

BACK

$6\frac{1}{8}''$

$1\frac{1}{2}''$

$6\frac{1}{8}''$

$6\frac{1}{8}''$

$1\frac{1}{2}$

6

SCALE IN INCHES

SEWING DESK
THE SHAKER MUSEUM, OLD CHATHAM, N.Y.

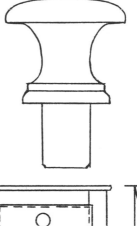

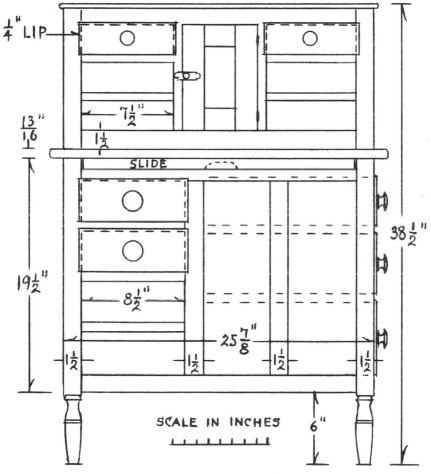

$\frac{1}{4}$" LIP

$7\frac{1}{2}$"

$\frac{13}{16}$"

$1\frac{1}{2}$

SLIDE

$8\frac{1}{2}$"

$19\frac{1}{2}$"

$25\frac{7}{8}$"

$38\frac{1}{2}$"

$1\frac{1}{2}$

$1\frac{1}{2}$

$1\frac{1}{2}$

$1\frac{1}{2}$

SCALE IN INCHES

6"

PINE
SEWING DESK

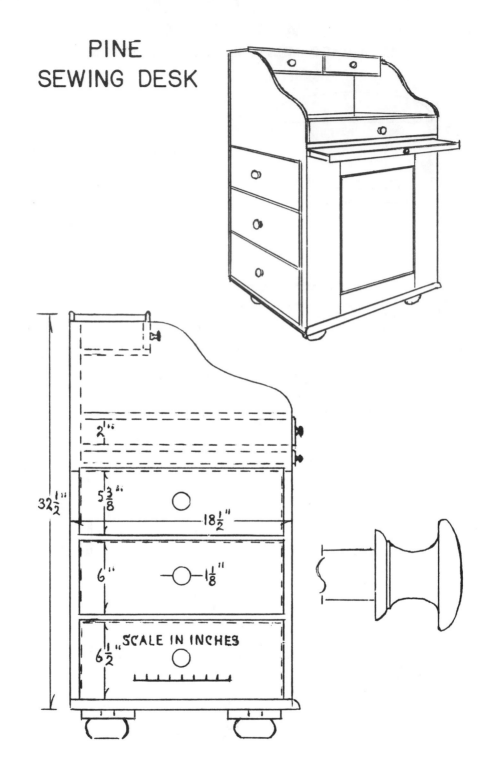

$32\frac{1}{2}''$

$2\frac{1}{4}''$

$5\frac{3}{8}''$

$18\frac{1}{2}''$

$6''$ $1\frac{1}{8}''$

$6\frac{1}{2}''$

SCALE IN INCHES

PINE SEWING DESK

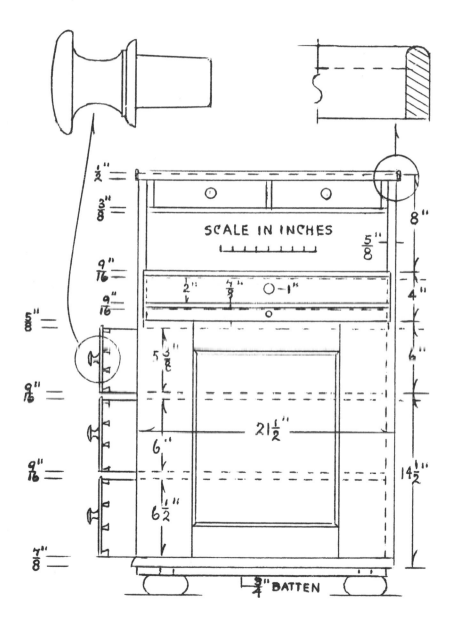

SCALE IN INCHES

8"

5/8"

4"

6"

14 1/2"

1/2"

3/8"

9/16"

9/16"

5/8"

9/16"

9/16"

7/8"

5 5/8"

6"

6 1/2"

21 1/2"

2"

7/8"

O — 1"

3/4" BATTEN

SEWING TABLE
THE SHAKER MUSEUM, OLD CHATHAM, N.Y.
CHERRY WITH PINE TOP

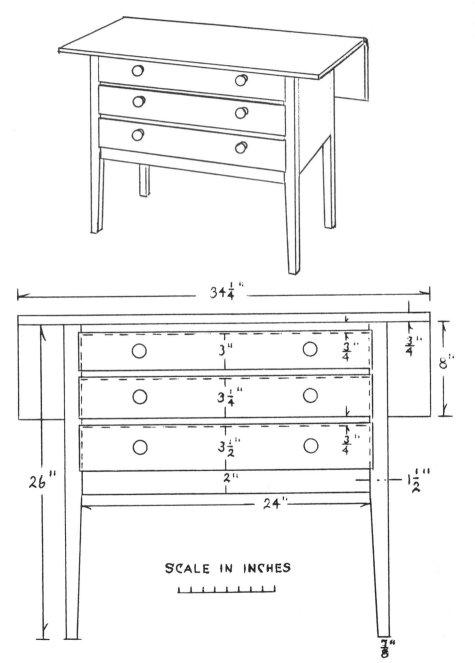

SCALE IN INCHES

SEWING TABLE

THE SHAKER MUSEUM, OLD CHATHAM, N. Y.

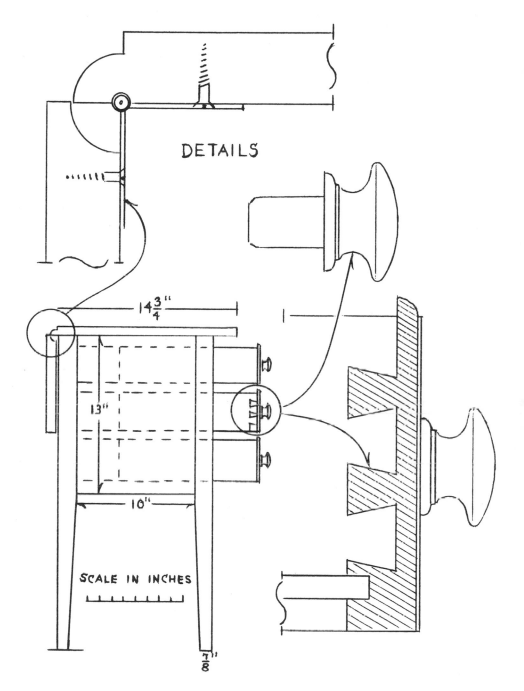

DETAILS

$14\frac{3}{4}"$

13"

10"

SCALE IN INCHES

$\frac{7}{8}"$

PINE TABLE
STAINED RED
FROM ANDREWS COLLECTION

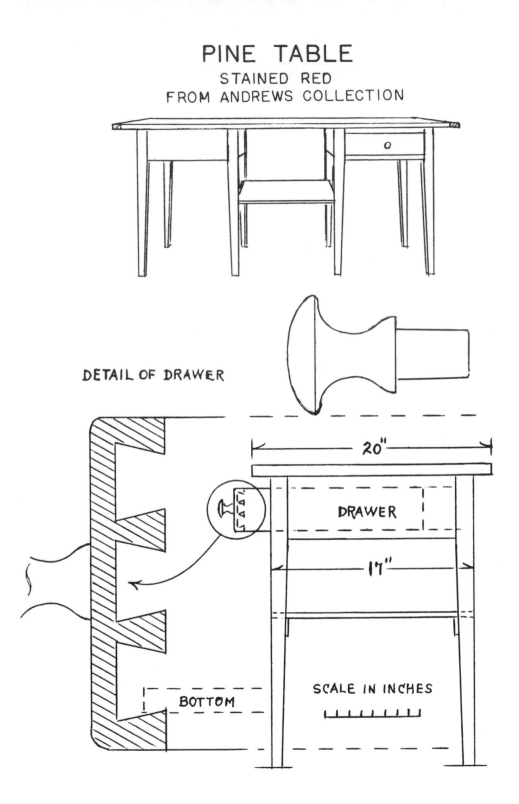

DETAIL OF DRAWER

20"

DRAWER

17"

BOTTOM

SCALE IN INCHES

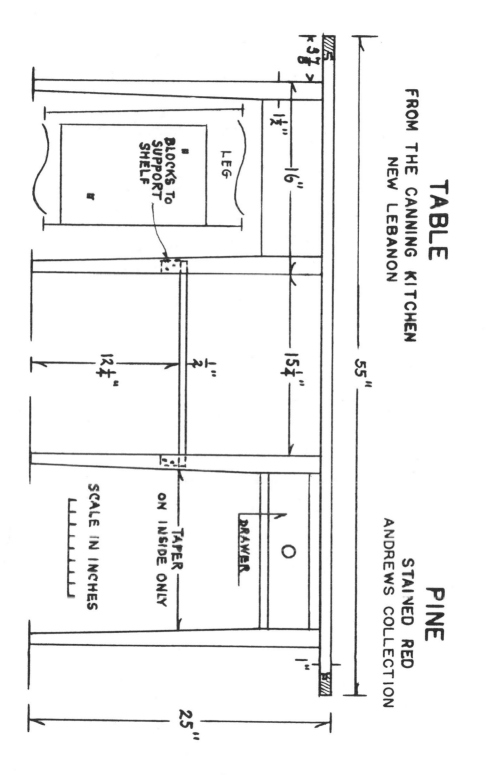

TABLE
FROM THE CANNING KITCHEN
NEW LEBANON

PINE
STAINED RED
ANDREWS COLLECTION

BLOCKS TO
SUPPORT
SHELF

LEG

TAPER
ON INSIDE ONLY

DRAWER

SCALE IN INCHES

$\frac{3}{8}$"

$1\frac{3}{4}$"

16"

55"

$15\frac{1}{4}$"

$12\frac{1}{4}$"

$\frac{1}{2}$"

1"

25"

BAKE-ROOM TABLE

FROM ANDREWS COLLECTION

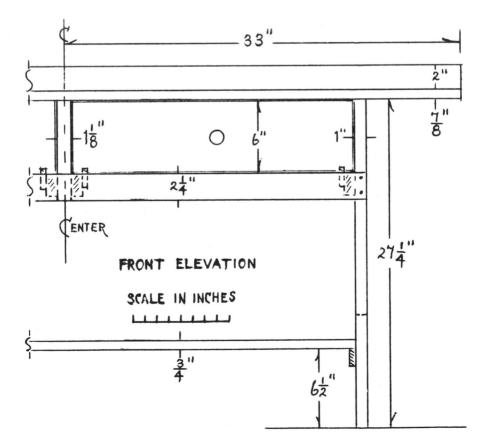

33"

2"

$\frac{7}{8}$"

$1\frac{1}{8}$"

6"

1"

$2\frac{1}{4}$"

CENTER

27$\frac{1}{4}$"

FRONT ELEVATION

SCALE IN INCHES

$\frac{3}{4}$"

6$\frac{1}{2}$"

BAKE-ROOM TABLE
FROM ANDREWS COLLECTION

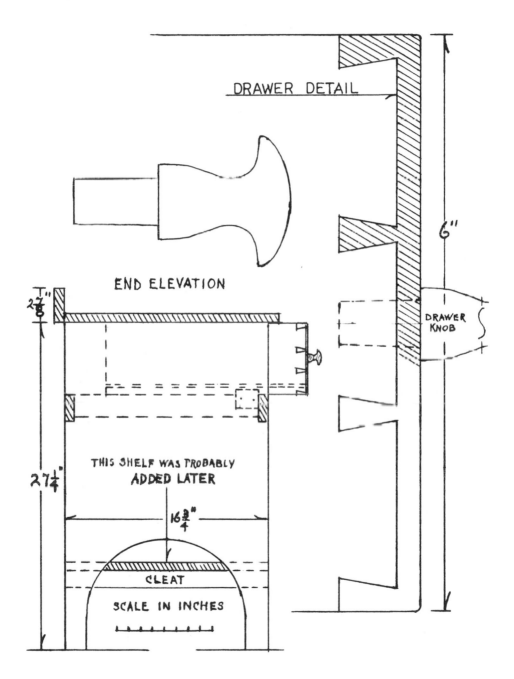

DRAWER DETAIL

END ELEVATION

6"

DRAWER KNOB

$2\frac{7}{8}$"

THIS SHELF WAS PROBABLY
ADDED LATER

$27\frac{1}{4}$"

$16\frac{3}{4}$"

CLEAT

SCALE IN INCHES

DROP-LEAF TABLE

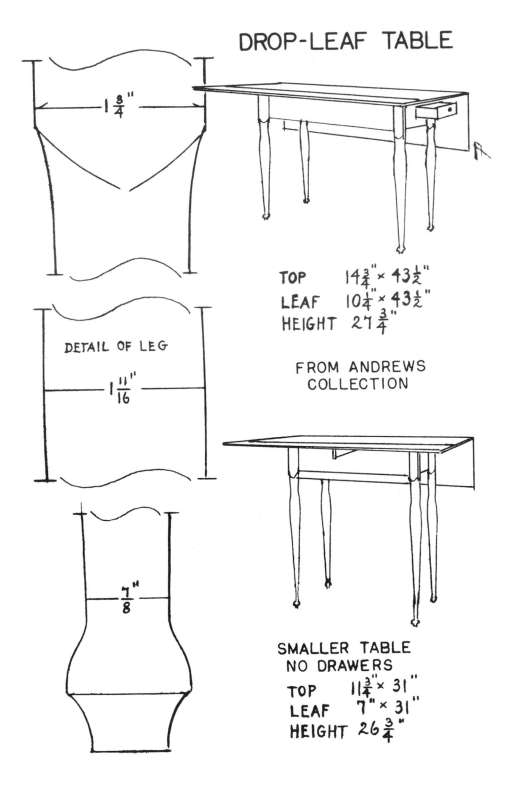

$1\frac{3}{4}''$

DETAIL OF LEG

$1\frac{11}{16}''$

$\frac{7}{8}''$

TOP $14\frac{3}{4}'' \times 43\frac{1}{2}''$
LEAF $10\frac{1}{4}'' \times 43\frac{1}{2}''$
HEIGHT $27\frac{3}{4}''$

FROM ANDREWS
COLLECTION

SMALLER TABLE
NO DRAWERS
TOP $11\frac{3}{4}'' \times 31''$
LEAF $7'' \times 31''$
HEIGHT $26\frac{3}{4}''$

18

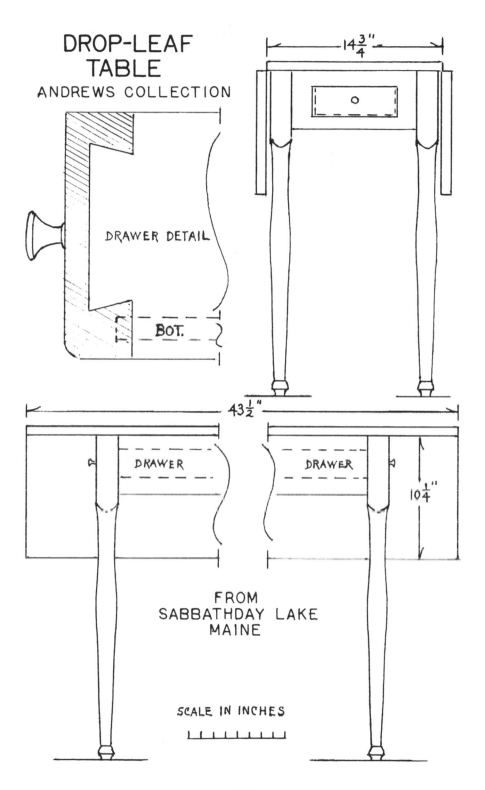

DROP-LEAF
TABLE
ANDREWS COLLECTION

14¾"

DRAWER DETAIL

BOT.

43½"

DRAWER

DRAWER

10¼"

FROM
SABBATHDAY LAKE
MAINE

SCALE IN INCHES

SMALL TABLE
LEGS OF CHERRY
TOP, FRAME AND DRAWER OF CHESTNUT

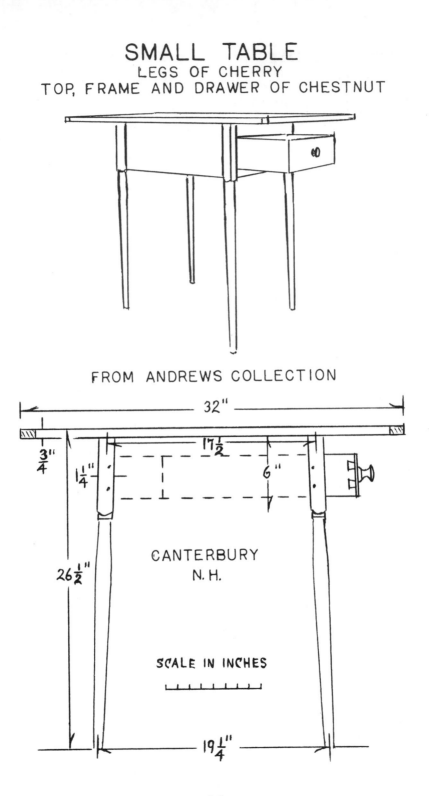

FROM ANDREWS COLLECTION

32"

3/4"

17½"

1¼"

6"

26½"

CANTERBURY
N. H.

SCALE IN INCHES

19¼"

20

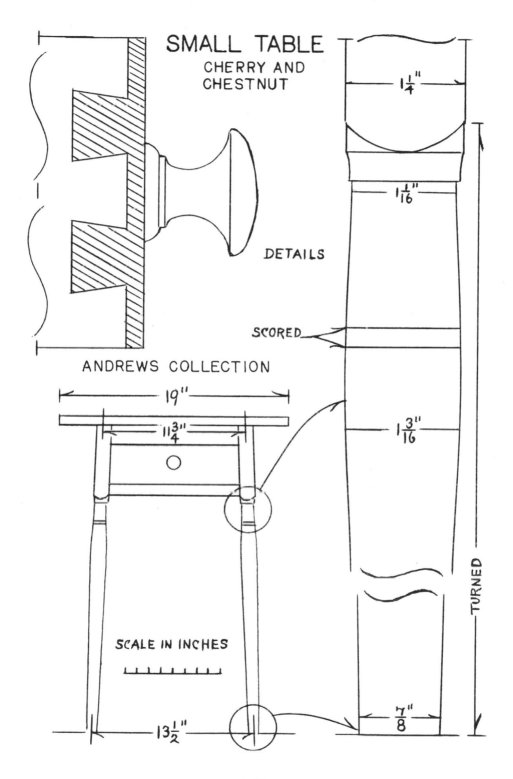

SMALL TABLE
CHERRY AND CHESTNUT

DETAILS

$1\frac{1}{4}$"

$1\frac{1}{16}$"

SCORED

$1\frac{3}{16}$"

ANDREWS COLLECTION

19"

$11\frac{3}{4}$"

SCALE IN INCHES

$13\frac{1}{2}$"

TURNED

$\frac{7}{8}$"

21

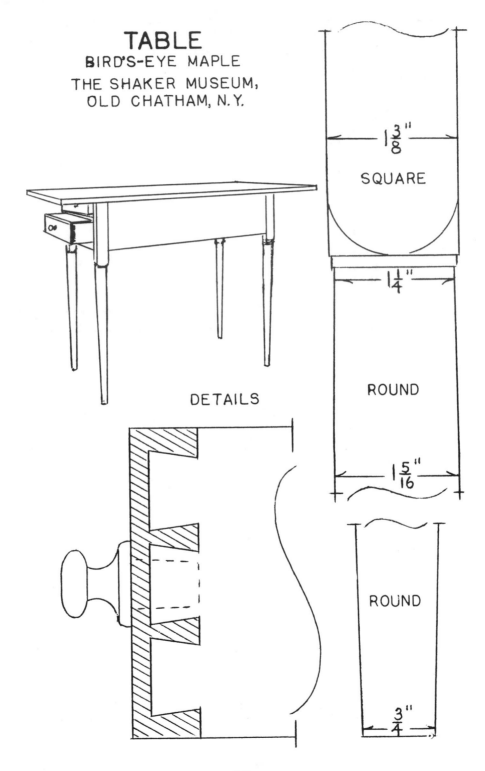

TABLE
BIRD'S-EYE MAPLE
THE SHAKER MUSEUM,
OLD CHATHAM, N.Y.

$1\frac{3}{8}"$

SQUARE

$1\frac{1}{4}"$

DETAILS

ROUND

$1\frac{5}{16}"$

ROUND

$\frac{3}{4}"$

22

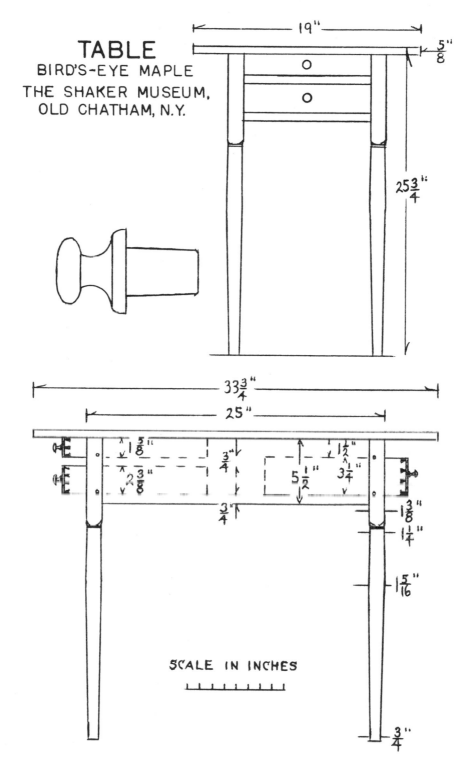

TABLE
BIRD'S-EYE MAPLE
THE SHAKER MUSEUM,
OLD CHATHAM, N.Y.

19"

$\frac{5}{8}$"

$25\frac{3}{4}$"

$33\frac{3}{4}$"

25"

$\frac{5}{8}$"

$2\frac{3}{8}$"

$\frac{3}{4}$"

$1\frac{1}{2}$"

$\frac{3}{4}$"

$5\frac{1}{2}$"

$3\frac{1}{4}$"

$\frac{3}{4}$"

$1\frac{3}{8}$"

$1\frac{1}{4}$"

$1\frac{5}{16}$"

$\frac{3}{4}$"

SCALE IN INCHES

23

PEG-LEG STAND

TOP $12\frac{1}{2}"\times18\frac{1}{2}"$

PINE TOP

BEVEL

$4\frac{1}{2}$

DETAILS

$4\frac{1}{4}"\times8\frac{1}{2}"\times9\frac{1}{2}"$

BACK

FLUSH DRAWER

PINE

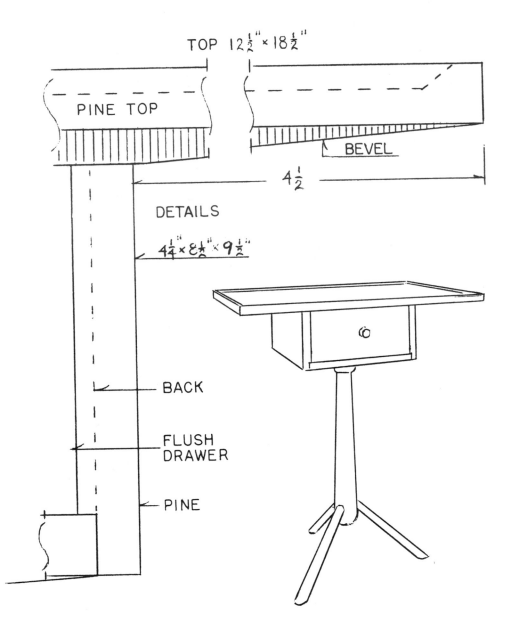

PEG-LEG STAND

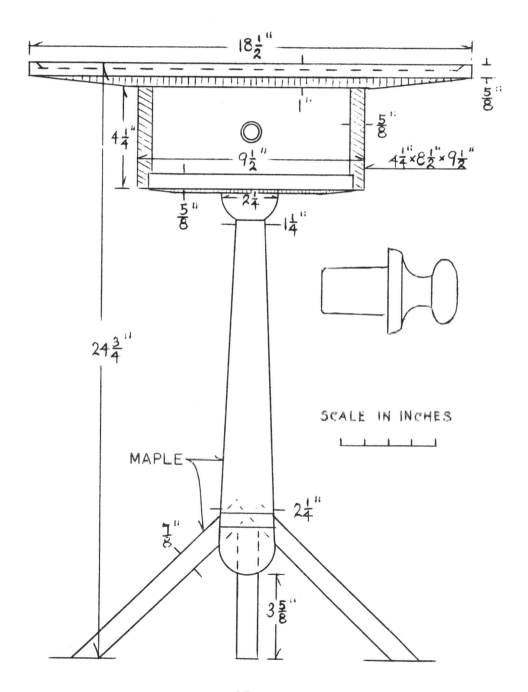

$18\frac{1}{2}"$

$\frac{1}{5}\frac{5}{8}"$

$1"$

$\frac{5}{8}"$

$4\frac{1}{4}"$

$9\frac{1}{2}"$

$4\frac{1}{4}"\times 8\frac{1}{2}"\times 9\frac{1}{2}"$

$\frac{5}{8}"$

$2\frac{1}{4}$

$1\frac{1}{4}"$

$24\frac{3}{4}"$

SCALE IN INCHES

MAPLE

$2\frac{1}{4}"$

$3\frac{7}{8}"$

$3\frac{5}{8}"$

DETAIL OF SHAFT

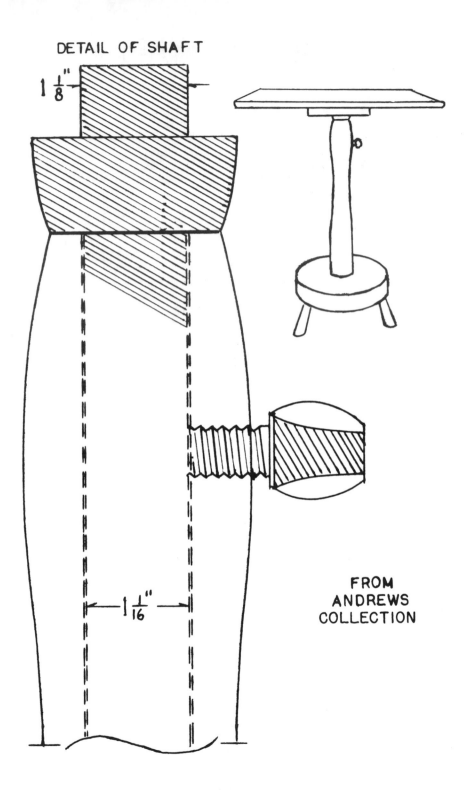

$1\frac{1}{8}$"

$1\frac{1}{16}$"

FROM
ANDREWS
COLLECTION

26

EARLY STAND
WITH ADJUSTABLE TOP

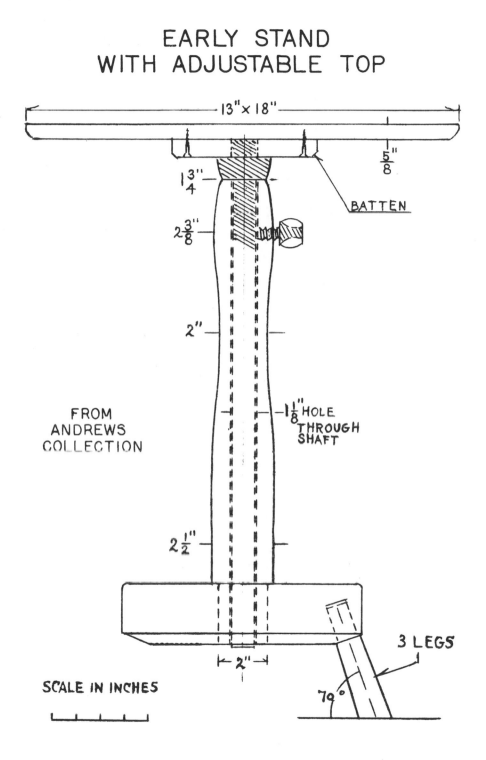

13" × 18"

5/8"

BATTEN

1 3/4"

2 3/8"

2"

FROM
ANDREWS
COLLECTION

1 1/8" HOLE
THROUGH
SHAFT

2 1/2"

3 LEGS

2"

79°

SCALE IN INCHES

27

STAND WITH ADJUSTABLE TOP
MAPLE AND PINE

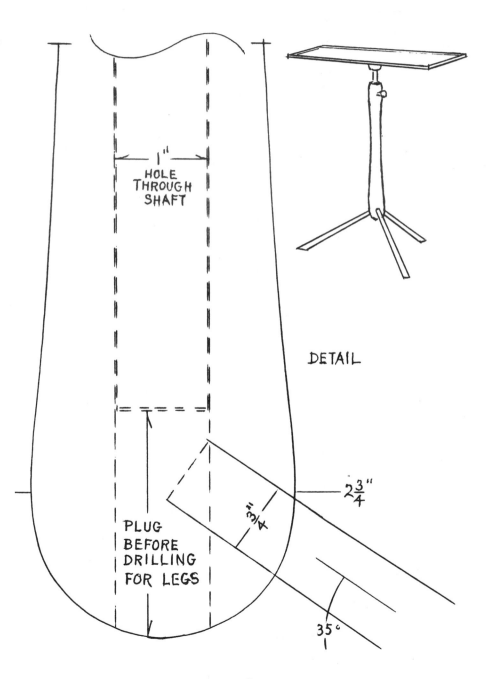

1"
HOLE
THROUGH
SHAFT

DETAIL

PLUG
BEFORE
DRILLING
FOR LEGS

$2\frac{3}{4}$"

$\frac{3}{4}$"

35°

STAND WITH ADJUSTABLE TOP
SHAFT AND LEGS OF MAPLE TOP OF PINE

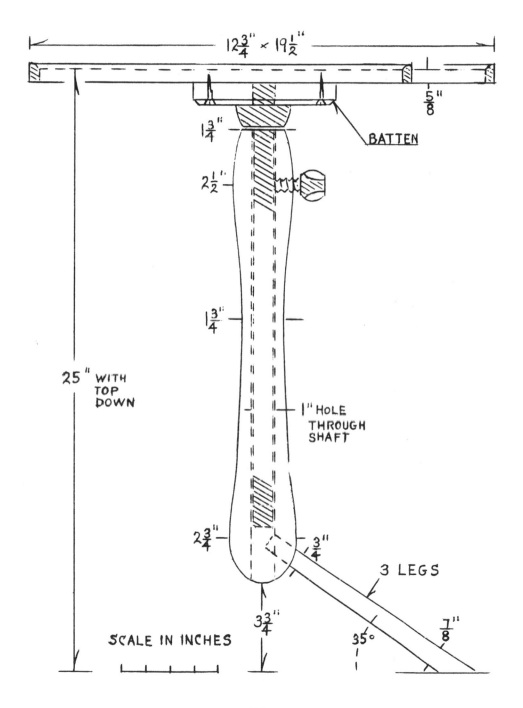

$12\frac{3}{4}'' \times 19\frac{1}{2}''$

$\frac{5}{8}''$

BATTEN

$1\frac{3}{4}''$

$2\frac{1}{2}''$

$1\frac{3}{4}''$

1" HOLE THROUGH SHAFT

25" WITH TOP DOWN

$2\frac{3}{4}''$

$\frac{3}{4}''$

3 LEGS

$\frac{7}{8}''$

$3\frac{3}{4}''$

35°

SCALE IN INCHES

WASHSTAND

PINE WITH
CHERRY LEGS

FROM ANDREWS
COLLECTION

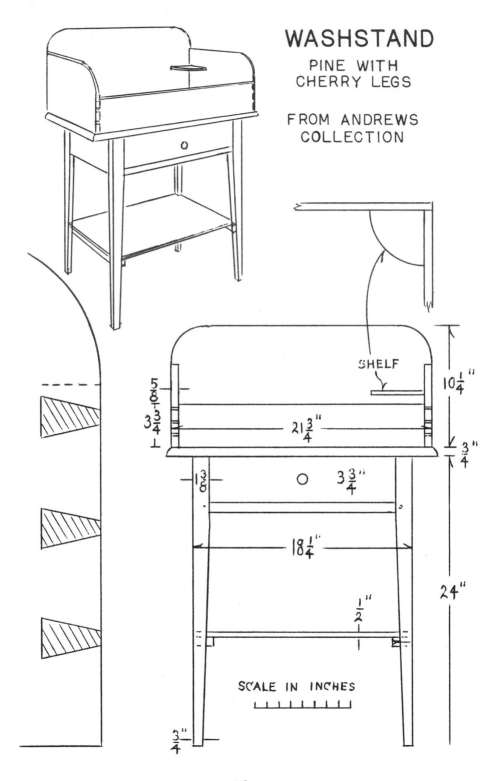

SHELF

$10\frac{1}{4}$"

$5\frac{1}{8}$
$3\frac{3}{8}$
$3\frac{3}{4}$

$21\frac{3}{4}$"

$\frac{3}{4}$"

$1\frac{3}{8}$

$3\frac{3}{4}$"

$18\frac{1}{4}$"

24"

$\frac{1}{2}$"

SCALE IN INCHES

$\frac{3}{4}$"

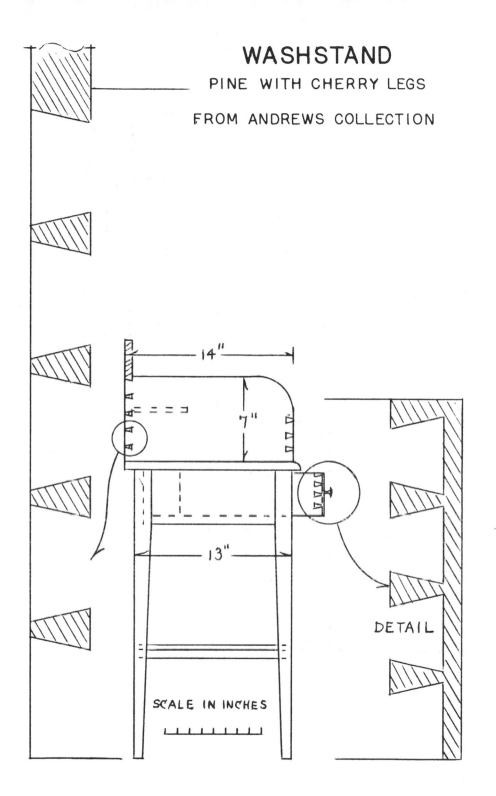

WASHSTAND

PINE WITH CHERRY LEGS

FROM ANDREWS COLLECTION

14"

7"

13"

DETAIL

SCALE IN INCHES

31

WASHSTAND

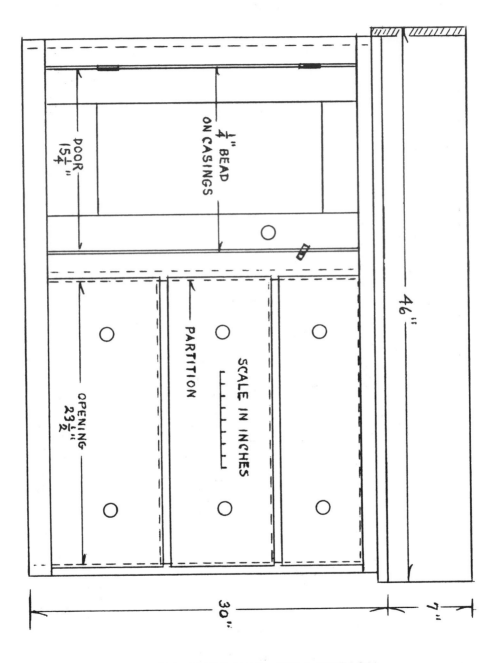

DOOR
$15\frac{1}{4}$"

$\frac{1}{4}$"
BEAD
ON CASINGS

46"

PARTITION

OPENING
$23\frac{1}{2}$"

SCALE IN INCHES

30"

7"

FROM ANDREWS COLLECTION

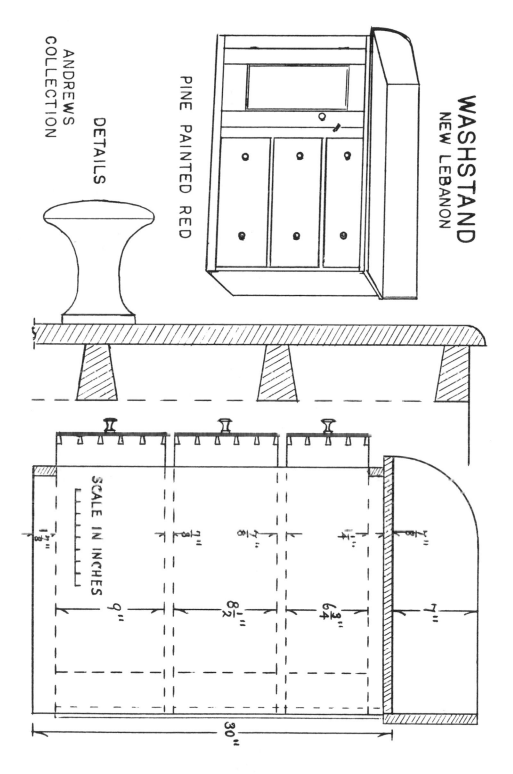

WASHSTAND
NEW LEBANON

PINE PAINTED RED

DETAILS

ANDREWS
COLLECTION

SCALE IN INCHES

$\frac{1}{8}$"

$\frac{7}{8}$"

$\frac{7}{8}$"

$\frac{1}{4}$"

$\frac{5}{8}$"

$1\frac{3}{8}$"

9"

$8\frac{1}{2}$"

$6\frac{3}{4}$"

7"

30"

BLANKET CHEST
PINE PAINTED RED

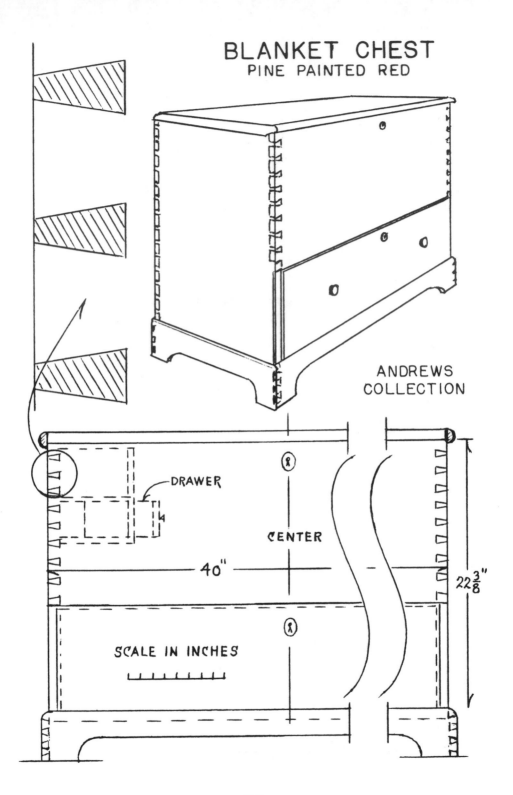

ANDREWS
COLLECTION

DRAWER

CENTER

40"

22$\frac{3}{8}$"

SCALE IN INCHES

34

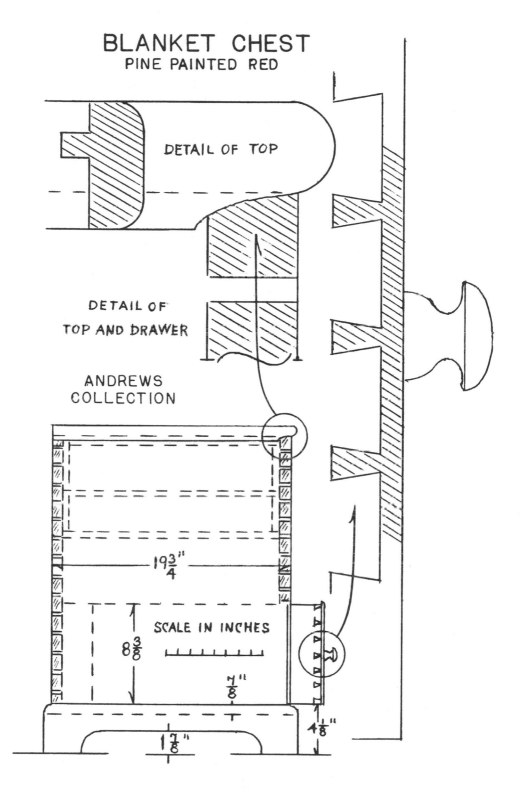

BLANKET CHEST
PINE PAINTED RED

DETAIL OF TOP

DETAIL OF
TOP AND DRAWER

ANDREWS
COLLECTION

$19\frac{3}{4}$"

$8\frac{3}{8}$

SCALE IN INCHES

$\frac{7}{8}$"

$1\frac{7}{8}$"

$4\frac{1}{8}$"

WOOD-BOX
PINE, STAINED RED

FROM
ANDREWS
COLLECTION

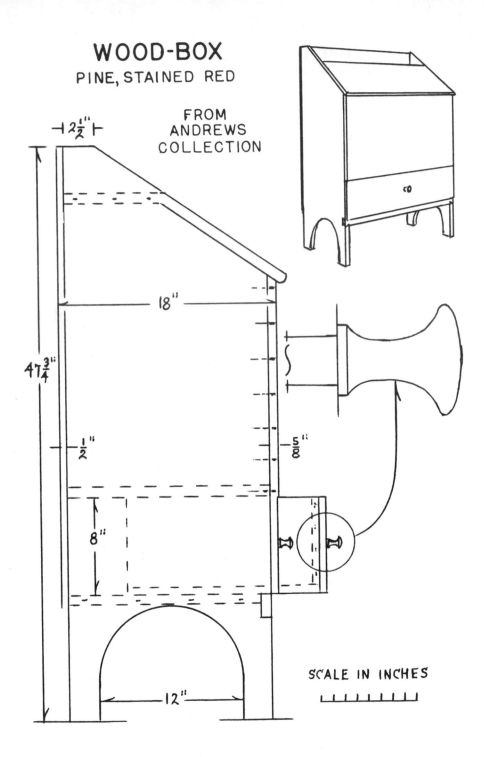

$2\frac{1}{2}''$

$47\frac{3}{4}''$

$18''$

$\frac{1}{2}''$

$\frac{5}{8}''$

$8''$

$12''$

SCALE IN INCHES

WOOD-BOX

MADE FOR THE MINISTRY CANTERBURY N.H.

FROM ANDREWS COLLECTION

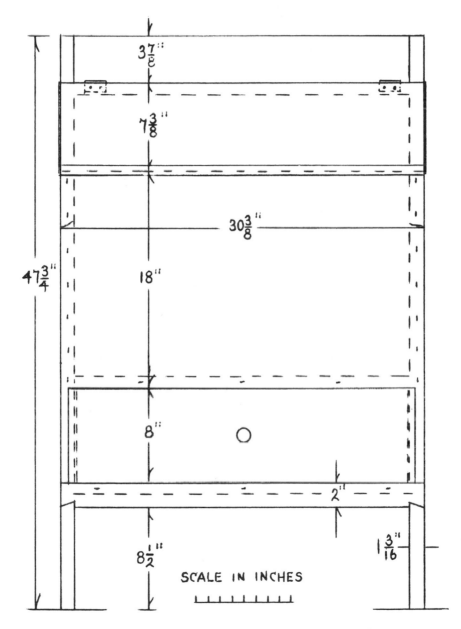

2 DRAWER UTILITY CHEST

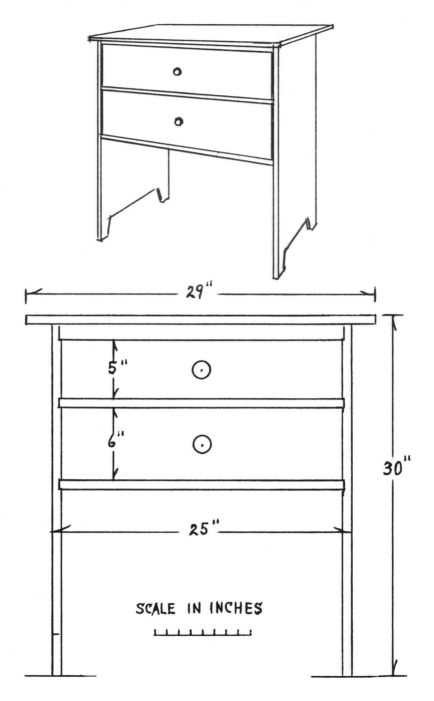

29"

5"

6"

30"

25"

SCALE IN INCHES

2 DRAWER UTILITY CHEST

FROM ANDREWS COLLECTION

DETAILS

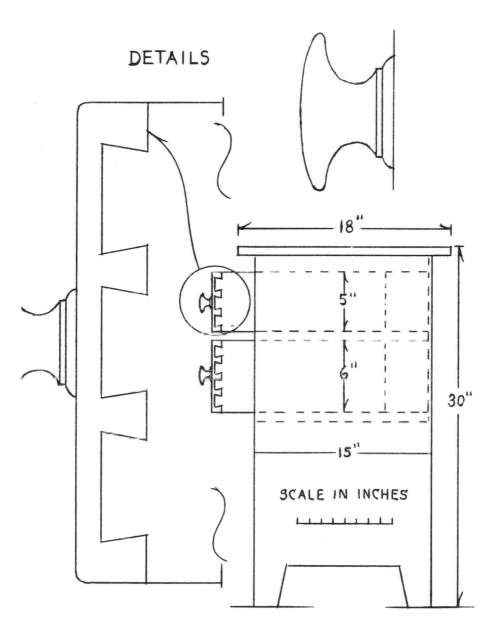

18"

5"

6"

30"

15"

SCALE IN INCHES

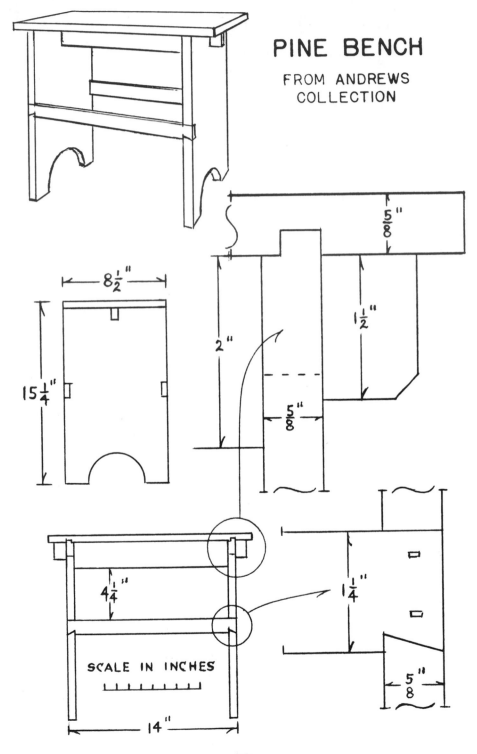

PINE BENCH

FROM ANDREWS
COLLECTION

$8\frac{1}{2}$"

$15\frac{1}{4}$"

$\frac{5}{8}$"

$1\frac{1}{2}$"

2"

$\frac{5}{8}$"

$4\frac{1}{4}$"

$1\frac{1}{4}$"

$\frac{5}{8}$

SCALE IN INCHES

14"

KITCHEN BENCH
HANCOCK SHAKER VILLAGE, HANCOCK MASS.

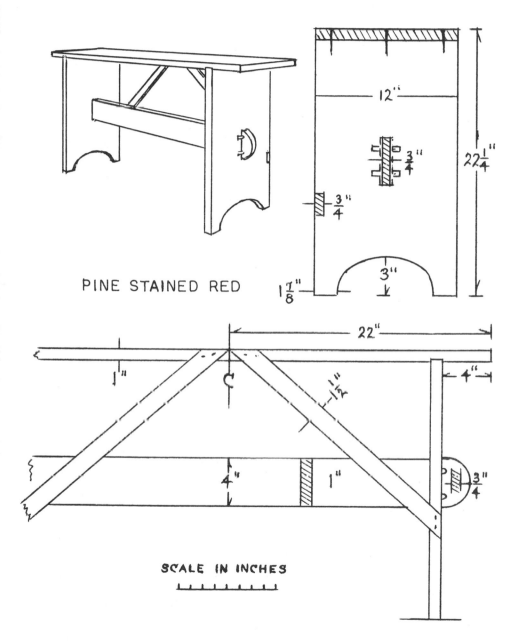

PINE STAINED RED

SCALE IN INCHES

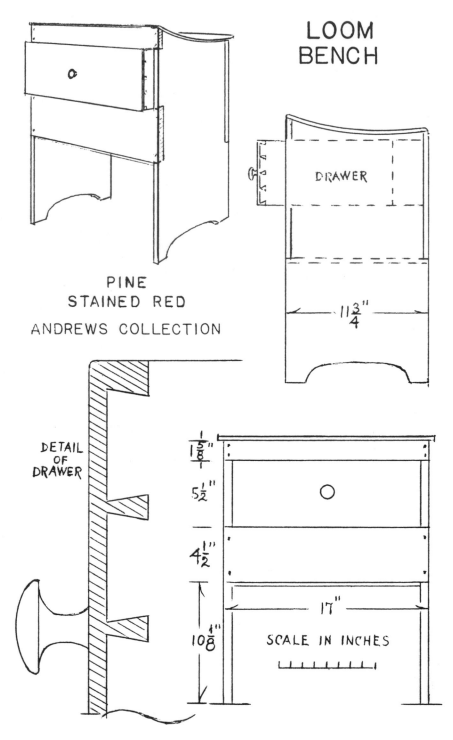

LOOM BENCH

PINE
STAINED RED

ANDREWS COLLECTION

DRAWER

$11\frac{3}{4}$"

DETAIL
OF
DRAWER

$1\frac{5}{8}$"

$5\frac{1}{2}$"

$4\frac{1}{2}$"

$10\frac{1}{8}$"

17"

SCALE IN INCHES

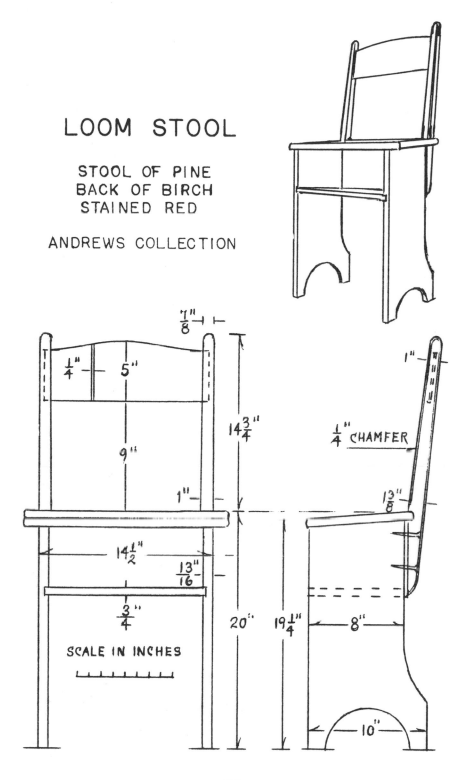

LOOM STOOL

STOOL OF PINE
BACK OF BIRCH
STAINED RED

ANDREWS COLLECTION

$\frac{7}{8}''$

$\frac{1}{4}''$ 5''

$14\frac{3}{4}''$

$\frac{1}{4}''$ CHAMFER

1''

9''

$1\frac{3}{8}''$

1''

$14\frac{1}{2}''$

$\frac{13}{16}$

$\frac{3}{4}''$

20''

$19\frac{1}{4}''$

8''

SCALE IN INCHES

10''

43

STEP-STOOL

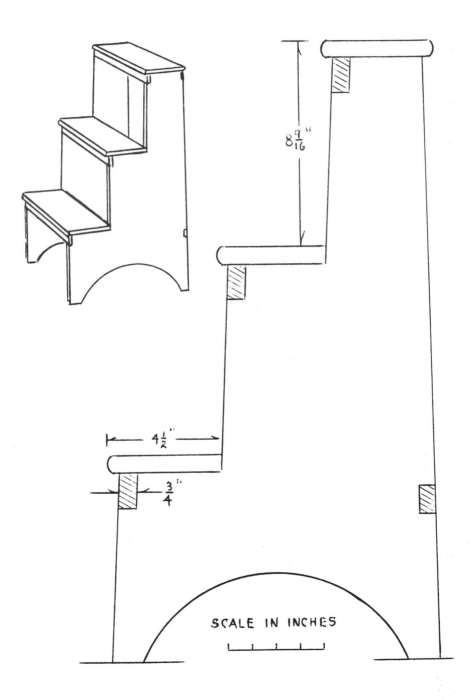

$8\frac{9}{16}"$

$4\frac{1}{2}"$

$\frac{3}{4}"$

SCALE IN INCHES

STEP-STOOL

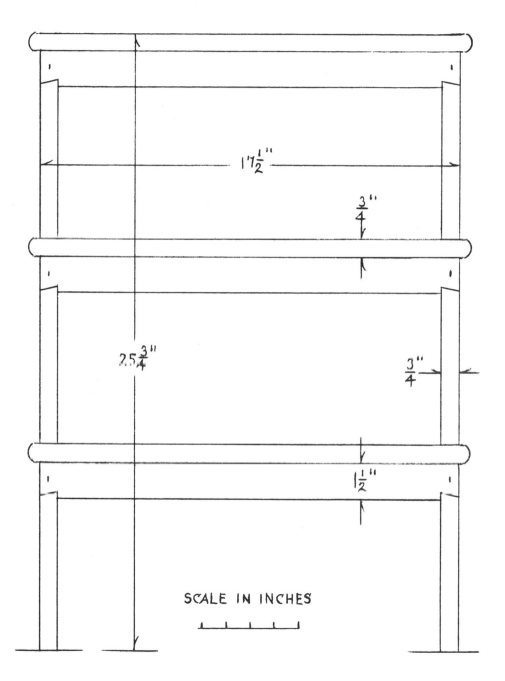

SCALE IN INCHES

REVOLVING STOOL

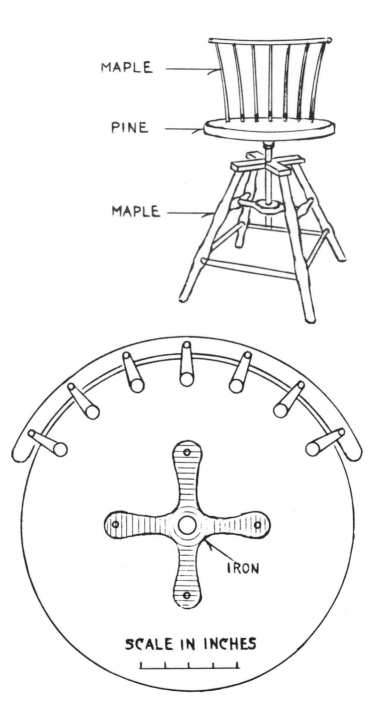

MAPLE

PINE

MAPLE

IRON

SCALE IN INCHES

REVOLVING STOOL

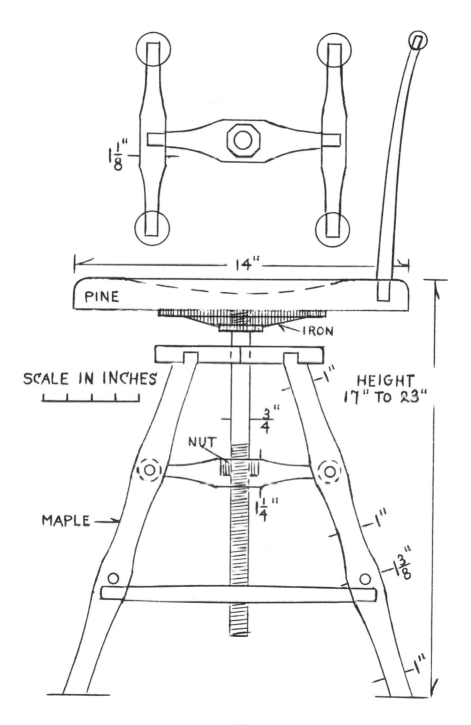

1⅛"

14"

PINE

IRON

SCALE IN INCHES

HEIGHT
17" TO 23"

1"

¾"

NUT

1¼"

MAPLE

1"

1⅜"

1"

STOOL MT. LEBANON

THE SHAKER MUSEUM
OLD CHATHAM, N.Y.

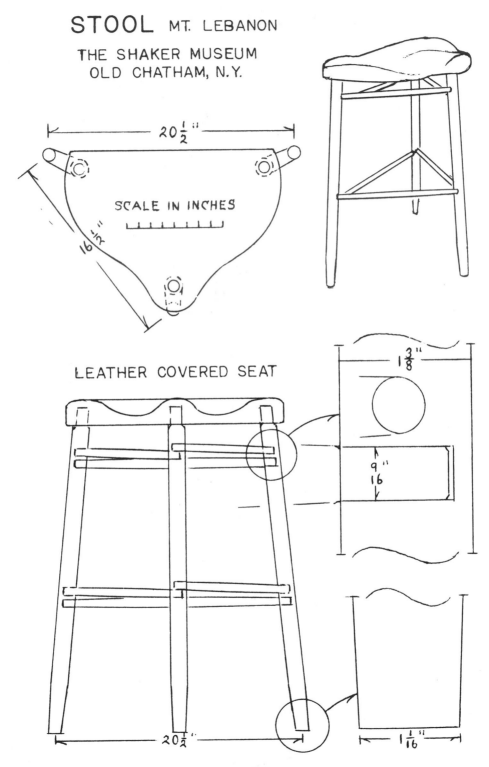

20½"

16½"

SCALE IN INCHES

LEATHER COVERED SEAT

1 3/8"

9/16"

1 1/16"

20½"

48

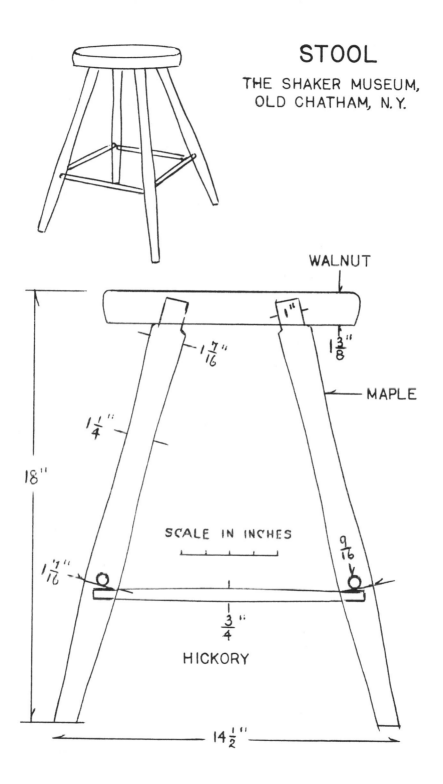

STOOL

THE SHAKER MUSEUM, OLD CHATHAM, N.Y.

WALNUT

$1''$

$1\frac{3}{8}''$

$1\frac{7}{16}''$

MAPLE

$1\frac{1}{4}''$

$18''$

SCALE IN INCHES

$\frac{9}{16}$

$1\frac{7}{16}''$

$\frac{3}{4}''$

HICKORY

$14\frac{1}{2}''$

ELDER ROBERT M. WAGAN
CHAIRMAKER

Illustrated Catalogue

AND

PRICE LIST

OF

Shakers' ✻ Chairs,

MANUFACTURED BY THE

Society ✻ of ✻ Shakers.

R. M. WAGAN & CO,

MOUNT LEBANON, N. Y.

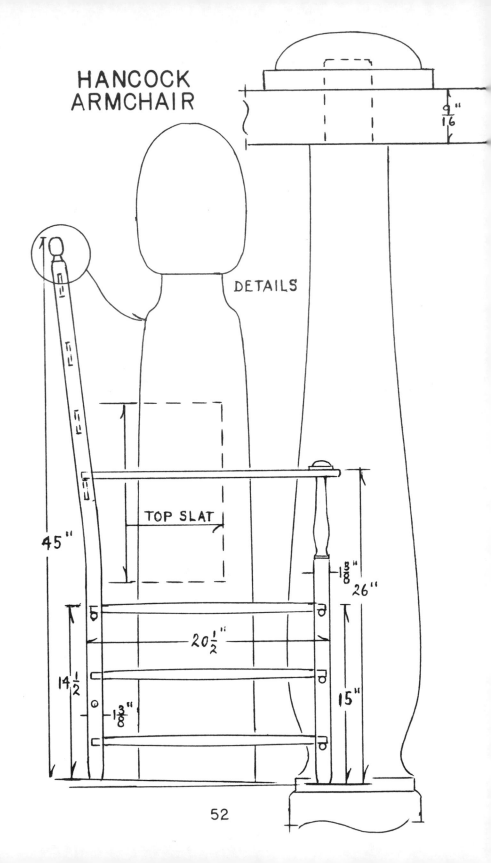

HANCOCK
ARMCHAIR

DETAILS

$\frac{9}{16}$"

TOP SLAT

45"

$1\frac{3}{8}$"

26"

$20\frac{1}{2}$"

$14\frac{1}{2}$

$1\frac{3}{8}$"

15"

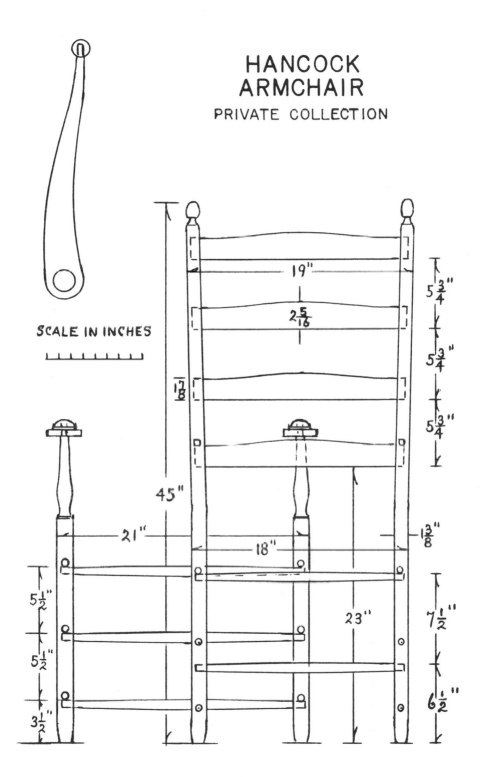

HANCOCK
ARMCHAIR
PRIVATE COLLECTION

SCALE IN INCHES

19"

$2\frac{5}{16}$

$5\frac{3}{4}$"

$5\frac{3}{4}$"

$5\frac{3}{4}$"

$1\frac{7}{8}$

45"

21"

18"

$1\frac{3}{8}$"

23"

$7\frac{1}{2}$"

$5\frac{1}{2}$"

$5\frac{1}{2}$"

$3\frac{1}{2}$"

$6\frac{1}{2}$"

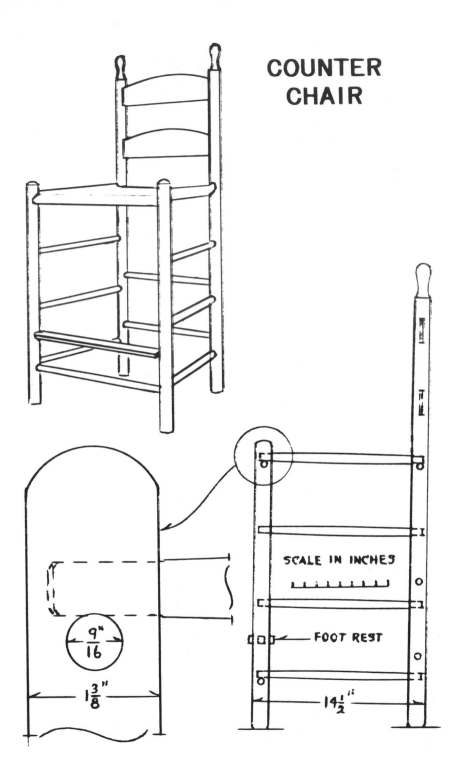

COUNTER
CHAIR

SCALE IN INCHES

FOOT REST

$\frac{9"}{16}$

$1\frac{3}{8}"$

$14\frac{1}{2}"$

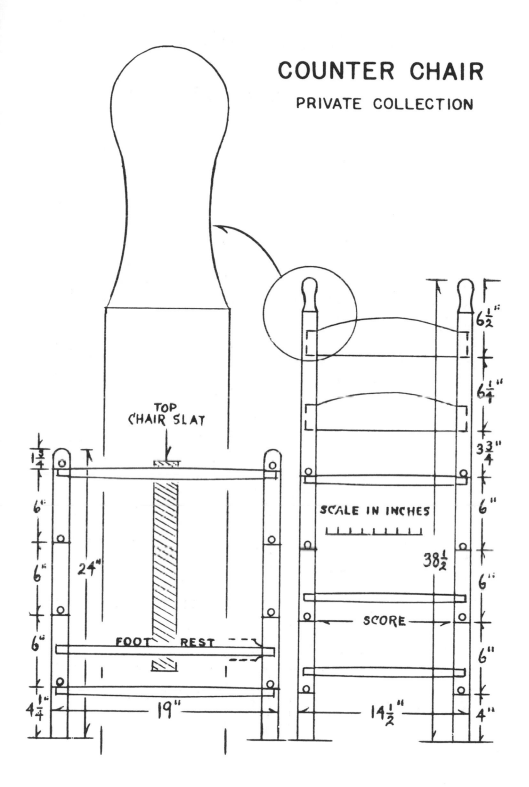

COUNTER CHAIR
PRIVATE COLLECTION

TOP
CHAIR SLAT

$1\frac{3}{4}$

$6"$

$6"$

$24"$

FOOT REST

$6"$

$4\frac{1}{4}"$

$19"$

$6\frac{1}{2}"$

$6\frac{1}{4}"$

$3\frac{3}{4}"$

$6"$

SCALE IN INCHES

$38\frac{1}{2}$

$6"$

SCORE

$6"$

$14\frac{1}{2}"$

$4"$

55

BRETHREN'S ROCKER
NEW LEBANON N.Y.

PRIVATE COLLECTION

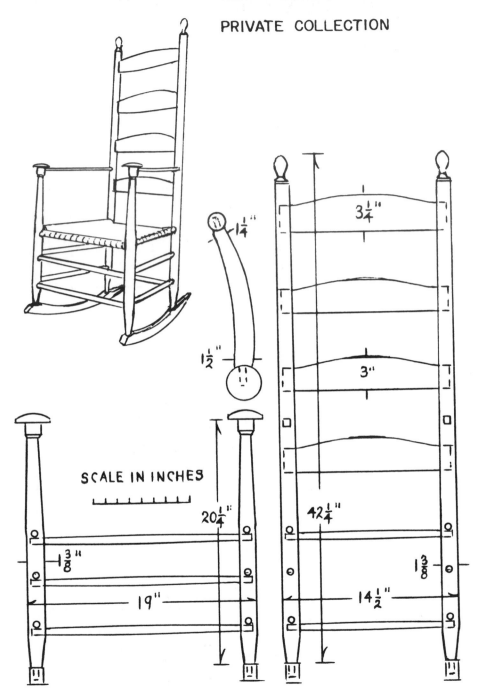

$3\frac{1}{4}$"

$1\frac{1}{4}$"

$1\frac{1}{2}$"

3"

SCALE IN INCHES

$20\frac{1}{4}$"

$42\frac{1}{4}$"

$1\frac{3}{8}$"

$1\frac{3}{8}$"

19"

$14\frac{1}{2}$"

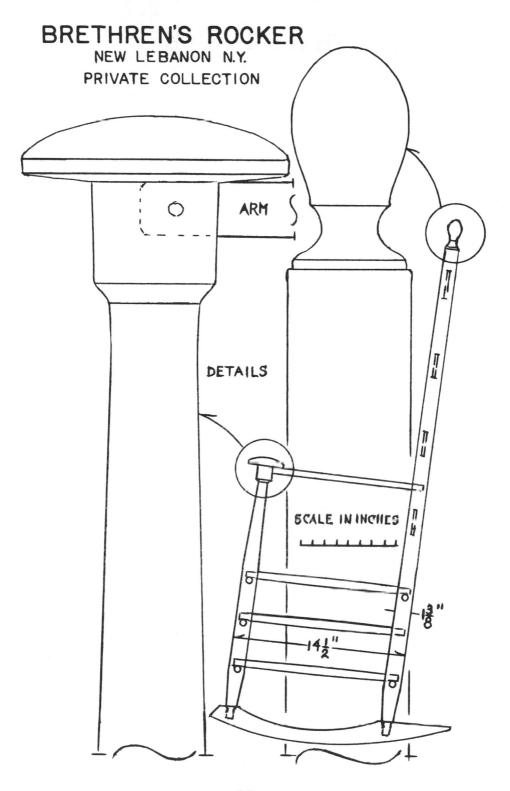

BRETHREN'S ROCKER
NEW LEBANON N.Y.
PRIVATE COLLECTION

ARM

DETAILS

SCALE IN INCHES

$14\frac{1}{2}$"

$\frac{3}{8}$"

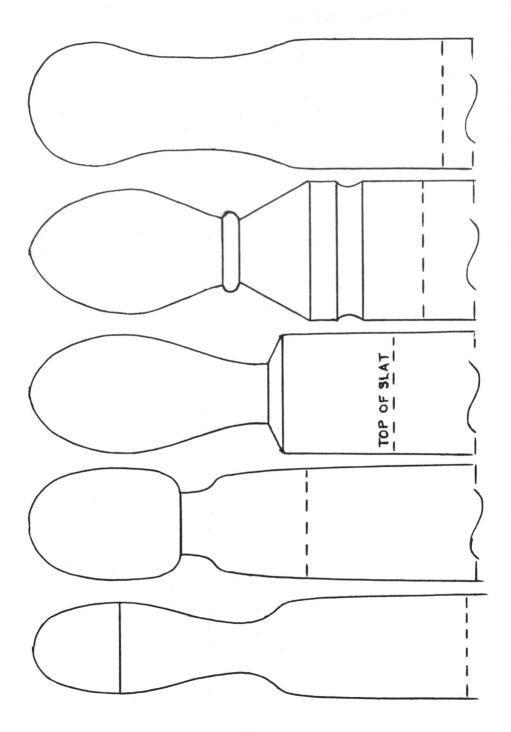

TOP OF SLAT

CHAIR MUSHROOMS
AND TILTING BUTTONS

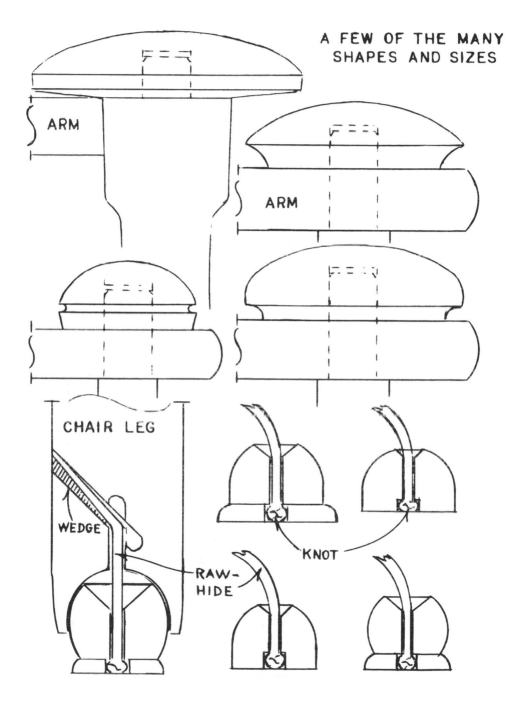

A FEW OF THE MANY
SHAPES AND SIZES

ARM

ARM

CHAIR LEG

WEDGE

RAW-
HIDE

KNOT

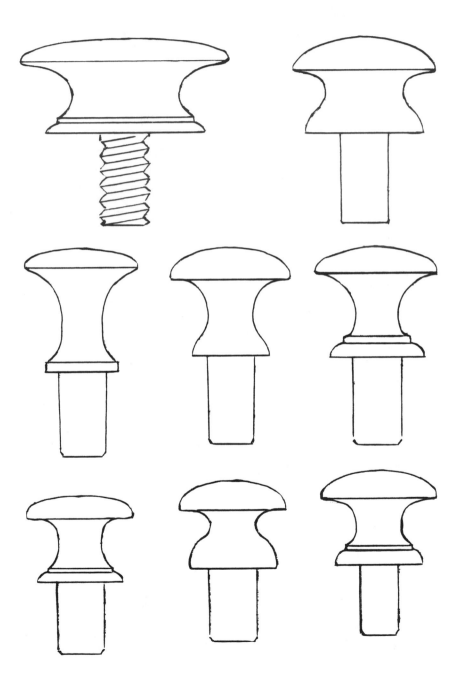

BED CASTERS

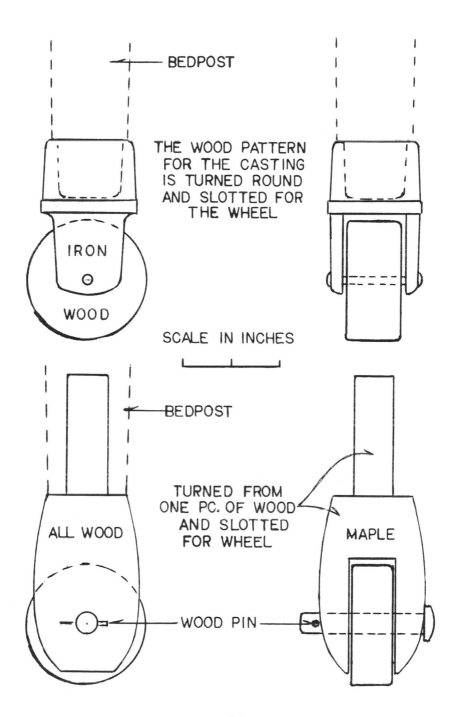

BEDPOST

THE WOOD PATTERN
FOR THE CASTING
IS TURNED ROUND
AND SLOTTED FOR
THE WHEEL

IRON

WOOD

SCALE IN INCHES

BEDPOST

TURNED FROM
ONE PC. OF WOOD
AND SLOTTED
FOR WHEEL

ALL WOOD

MAPLE

WOOD PIN

HANGING SHELF

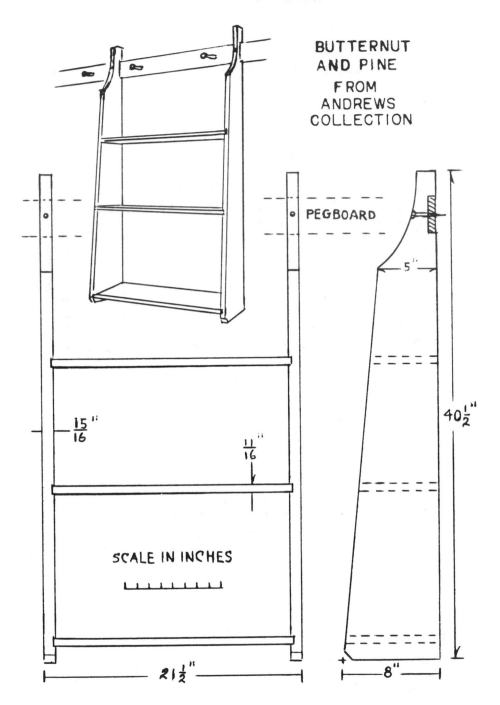

BUTTERNUT
AND PINE

FROM
ANDREWS
COLLECTION

PEGBOARD

5"

$40\frac{1}{2}$"

$\frac{15}{16}$"

$\frac{11}{16}$"

SCALE IN INCHES

$21\frac{1}{2}$"

8"

SMALL WALL CUPBOARD

HANCOCK SHAKER VILLAGE, HANCOCK MASS.

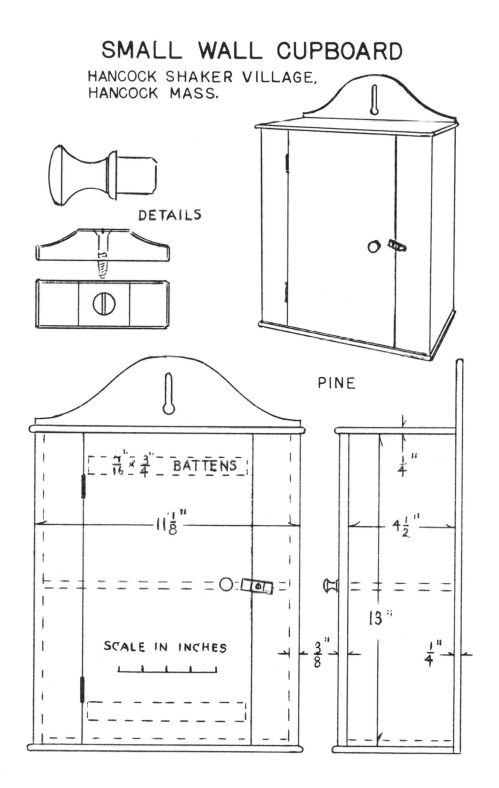

DETAILS

PINE

$\frac{7}{16}" \times \frac{3}{4}"$ BATTENS

$11\frac{1}{8}"$

$4\frac{1}{2}"$

$\frac{1}{4}"$

$13"$

$\frac{3}{8}"$

$\frac{1}{4}"$

SCALE IN INCHES

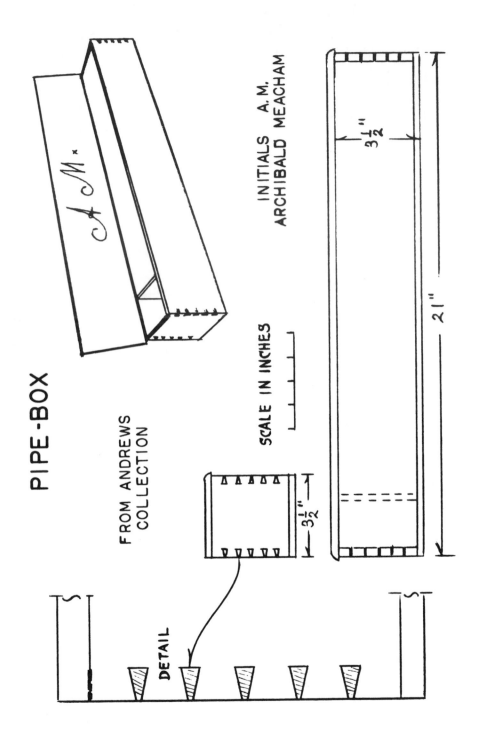

PIPE-BOX

FROM ANDREWS
COLLECTION

INITIALS A.M.
ARCHIBALD MEACHAM

SCALE IN INCHES

$3\frac{1}{2}$"

$3\frac{1}{2}$"

21"

DETAIL

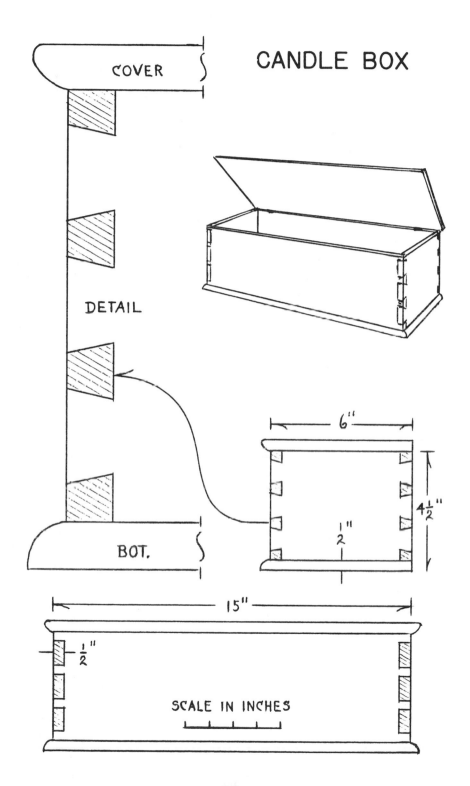

CANDLE BOX

COVER

DETAIL

BOT.

6"

4½"

½"

15"

½"

SCALE IN INCHES

65

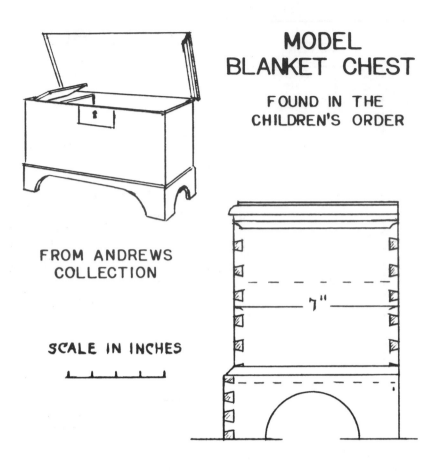

MODEL
BLANKET CHEST

FOUND IN THE
CHILDREN'S ORDER

FROM ANDREWS
COLLECTION

SCALE IN INCHES

7"

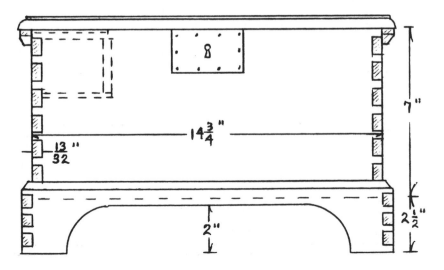

7"

$14\frac{3}{4}$"

$\frac{13}{32}$"

2"

$2\frac{1}{2}$"

WALNUT TRAY

NEW LEBANON, N.Y.   PRIVATE COLLECTION

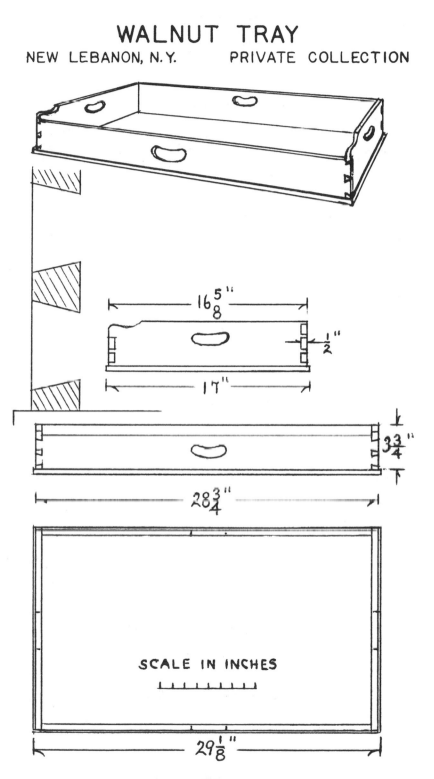

$16\frac{5}{8}$"

$\frac{1}{2}$"

17"

$3\frac{3}{4}$"

$28\frac{3}{4}$"

SCALE IN INCHES

$29\frac{1}{8}$"

SCOOP
PRIVATE COLLECTION

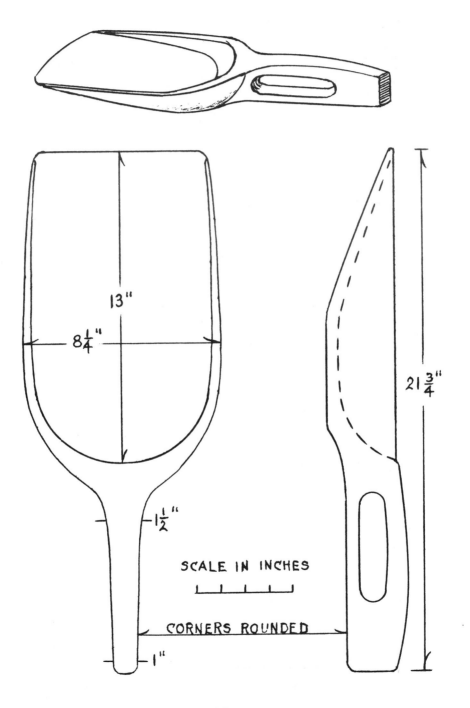

13"

8¼"

1½"

21¾"

SCALE IN INCHES

CORNERS ROUNDED

1"

MORTAR AND PESTLE
THE SHAKER MUSEUM, OLD CHATHAM, N.Y.

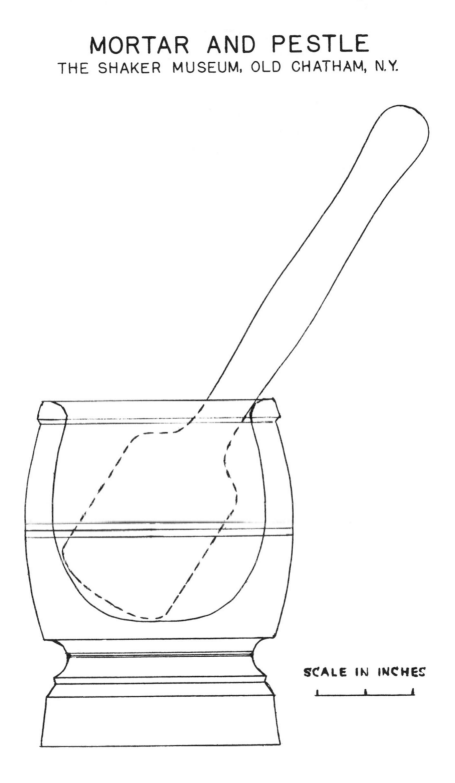

SCALE IN INCHES

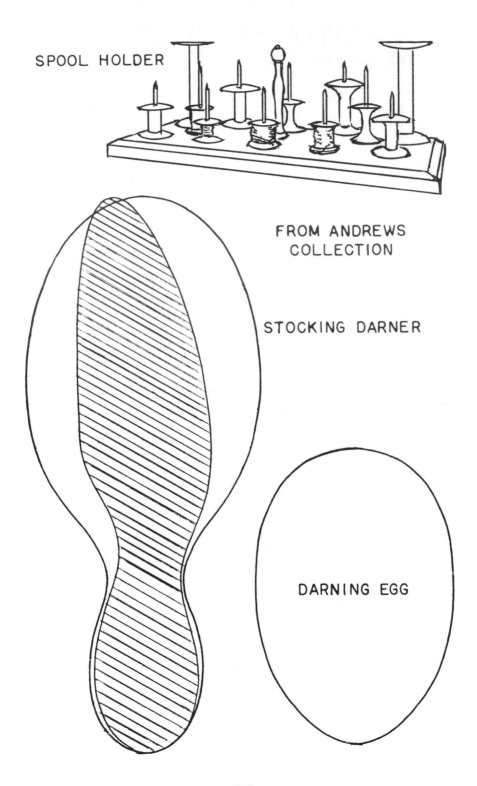

SPOOL HOLDER

FROM ANDREWS
COLLECTION

STOCKING DARNER

DARNING EGG

THUMB AND MITTEN DARNER

FROM
ANDREWS
COLLECTION

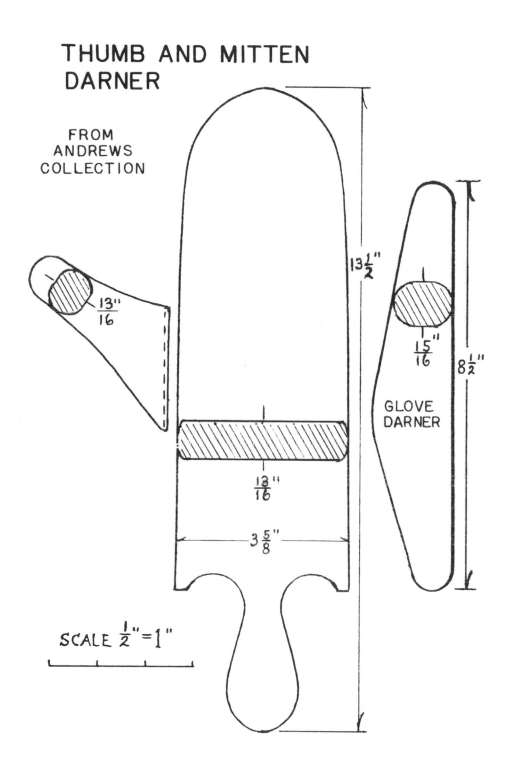

$13''/16$

$13\frac{1}{2}''$

$13''/16$

$3\frac{5}{8}''$

$15''/16$

$8\frac{1}{2}''$

GLOVE
DARNER

SCALE $\frac{1}{2}'' = 1''$

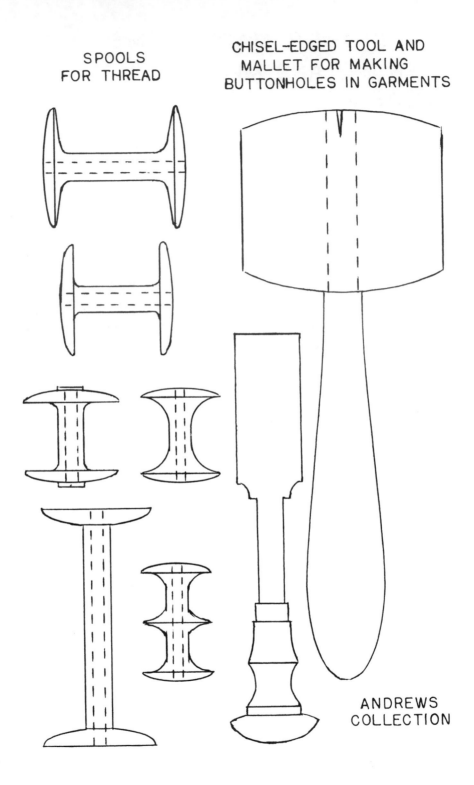

SPOOLS
FOR THREAD

CHISEL-EDGED TOOL AND
MALLET FOR MAKING
BUTTONHOLES IN GARMENTS

ANDREWS
COLLECTION

SHAKER MADE ITEMS

1 DARNER
2 BONNET PLEATER
3   "   "
4 SPOOL FOR THREAD

PRIVATE COLLECTION

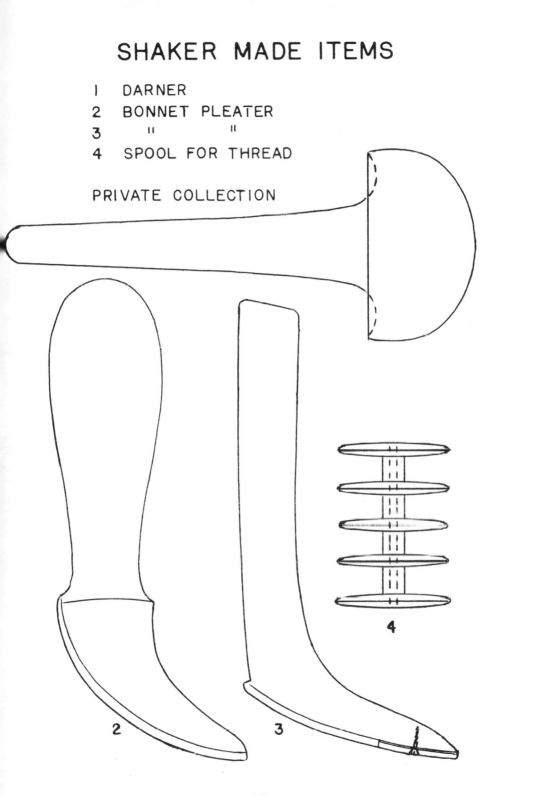

MT. LEBANON STOVE
DOUBLE FOR MORE EFFICIENT HEATING

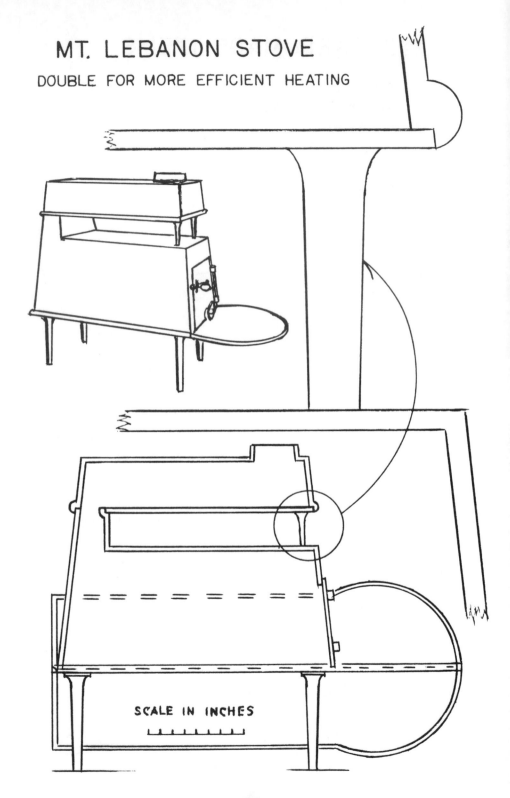

SCALE IN INCHES

MT. LEBANON STOVE

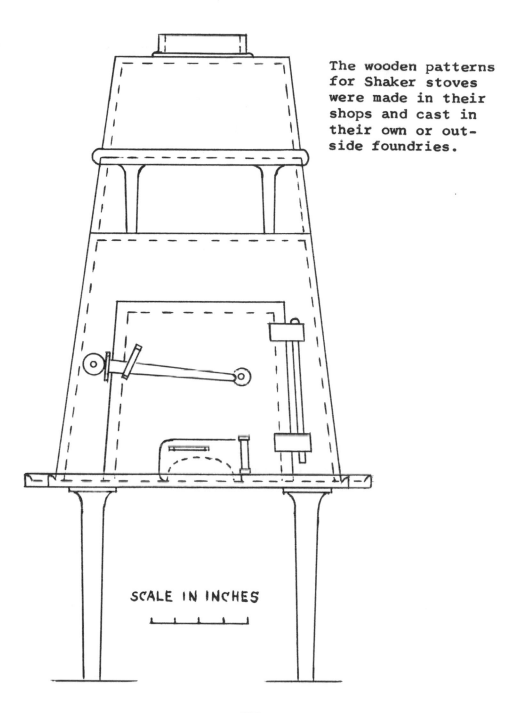

The wooden patterns
for Shaker stoves
were made in their
shops and cast in
their own or out-
side foundries.

SCALE IN INCHES

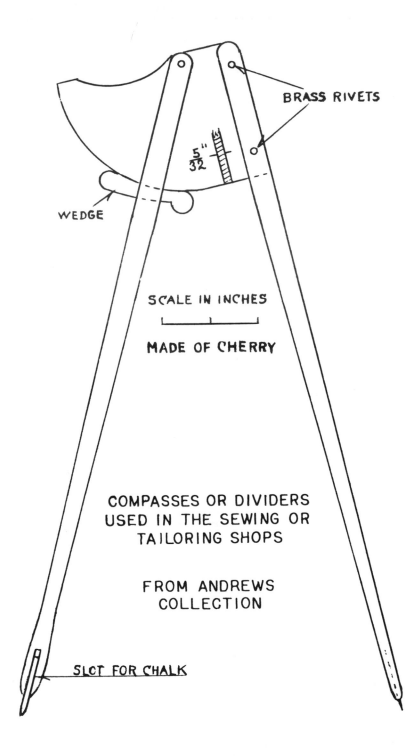

BRASS RIVETS

$\frac{5"}{32}$

WEDGE

SCALE IN INCHES

MADE OF CHERRY

COMPASSES OR DIVIDERS
USED IN THE SEWING OR
TAILORING SHOPS

FROM ANDREWS
COLLECTION

SLOT FOR CHALK

Washstand — page 33

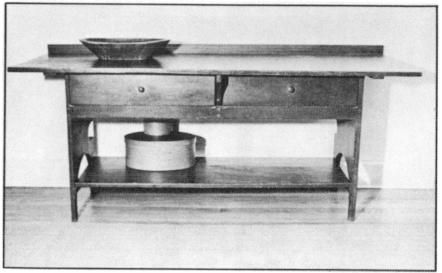

Bake-Room Table — page 16

Washstand — page 30

Dividers — page 76

Drop-Leaf Table — page 18

Pine Table — page 14

Blanket Chest — page 34

Desk — page 4

Pine Bench — page 40   Loom Bench — page 42

Spool Holder — page 70

ABOUT THE AUTHOR

This is the fourth book in the series on Shaker furniture and artifacts, by Ejner Handberg.

Mr. Handberg was a skilled cabinetmaker with more than fifty years experience who first became interested in Shaker furniture and design when people brought the vaulable Shaker pieces to him to repair or restore. Born in Denmark, he came to the U.S. at 17 years of age and learned his craft from 19th-century cabinetmakers who insisted upon precision and accuracy.

Volume I and II in this series on Shaker Furniture and Woodenware each contain meticulous drawings of many different types of Shaker chairs, boxes, tables, stools, knobs, candlesticks, trays, benches and similar pieces.

In Volume III, Mr. Handberg included many larger items, such as rocking chairs, tables, school desks, sewing stands, cupboards, a storage bench, a clock case, an upright desk, a dining table, a lantern, pine cupboards, a settee, and counters.

In these three books, as well as in Mr. Handberg's book of Shop Drawings of Shaker Iron and Tinware, he exercised extreme care to perfect measured drawings of these original Shaker pieces for the purpose of reproducing them in his own shop. Each drawing in every book is unique because it is carefully measured from an original Shaker piece. He followed as closely as possible the reverence that these unusual people had for wood and the purely functional purpose in furniture.

The informed amateur worker in wood, as well as the professional cabinetmaker and the enthusiastic collector, will find Mr. Handberg's books a valuable addition to the perpetuation of Shaker qualities.

INDEX

Asterisks after plate numbers refer to drawings made from pieces in the collection of Dr. and Mrs. Edward Deming Andrews.

BOOKS ON SHAKER FROM BERKSHIRE HOUSE, PUBLISHERS

By Ejner Handberg

Shop Drawings of Shaker Furniture and Woodenware, Vols. 1, 2, 3

Measured Drawings of Shaker Furniture and Woodenware

Field Guides to Shaker Antiques

Shaker Woodenware, Vol. 1

Shaker Woodenware, Vol. 2 (Spring 1992)

Shaker Baskets and Poplarware (Spring 1992)

Shaker Textiles, Costume and Fancy Goods (Forthcoming)

Shaker Paper (Forthcoming)

Shaker Iron, Tin, and Brass (Forthcoming)

Shaker Furniture (Forthcoming)

OTHER BOOKS FROM BERKSHIRE HOUSE

Travel: The Great Destinations Series

The Berkshire Book: A Complete Guide

The Santa Fe and Taos Book

The Napa and Sonoma Book

The Chesapeake Bay Book (Spring 1992)

The Coast of Maine Book (Spring 1992)

Recreation

Music Festivals in America

Yukon Wild

Berkshire Outdoors Series

Hikes & Walks in the Berkshire Hills

Skiing in the Berkshire Hills

Bike Rides in the Berkshire Hills